INTIMATIONS OF CHRISTIANITY AMONG THE ANCIENT GREEKS

Born in Paris in 1909, Simone Weil was educated at the Lycée Henri IV and the Ecole Normale Supérieure, where she was one of the first women students. She became a teacher, but also worked on farms and at the Renault car factory, choosing hard manual labour in order to experience the life of the working class with whom she had a profound sympathy. In 1936 she joined the Republican forces in the Spanish Civil War, returning from the front when she was badly burned in an accident. In 1938 she had the first of several mystical experiences which were deeply to affect her thought, although she was never received into the Catholic church. In 1942 Simone Weil left France and joined the Free French forces in London. She died there of tuberculosis the following year, refusing to eat more than the rations of those suffering Nazi occupation in her native France.

Simone Weil's writings reflect her intellectual and spiritual concerns: the nature of oppression, the reasons for human exploitation and, in the last years of her life, the relationship of the human condition to the realm of the transcendent. Her major works, published posthumously, include *Gravity and Grace* and *The Need for Roots*, also published by Routledge.

INTIMATIONS OF CHRISTIANITY AMONG THE ANCIENT GREEKS

Simone Weil

London and New York

This book consists of chapters from *La Source Grecque*
published in 1952 by Librairie Gallimard
and *Les Intuitions Pré-chrétiennes*
published in 1951 by Les Editions de la Colombe

This translation first published 1957
by Routledge
Reprinted 1976
Ark edition 1987

Reissued 1998 by Routledge
2 Park Square, Milton Park, Abingdon, Oxon, OX14 4RN
270 Madison Ave, New York NY 10016

Routledge is an imprint of the Taylor & Francis Group

Transferred to Digital Printing 2005

British Library Cataloguing in Publication Data
A catalogue record for this book is available from
the British Library

Library of Congress Cataloguing in Publication Data
Weil, Simone, 1909–1943
Intimations of Christianity among the Ancient Greeks /
Simone Weil.
p.   cm.
Consists of chapters from *La source grecque* and *Les intuitions
pré-chrétiennes*
Originally published: Boston : Beacon Press, 1957, c1957.
1. Philosophy, Ancient.   2. Christianity and other religions–Greek.
3. Greece–Religion.   I. Title.
B172.W34   1998
180–dc21   97–49211

ISBN 0–415–18662–5

EDITOR'S NOTE

THIS book is a collection of Simone Weil's writings on Greek thought. It is taken partly from *La Source Grecque* and from *Les Intuitions Pré-chrétiennes*, both of which were published posthumously.

Because Simone Weil's translations are as much a part of her whole view of Greek thought as her commentaries, we have attempted to render both as faithfully as possible.

CONTENTS

I

GOD'S QUEST FOR MAN[1]

'Quaerens me sedisti lassus. . . .'[2]
(Notice that in the Gospels there is never, unless I am mistaken,
question of a search for God by man. In all the parables it is the
Christ who seeks men, or else the Father has them fetched by
His messengers. Or again, a man finds the Kingdom of God as if
by chance, and then, but then only, he sells all.)

*   *   *

HOMERIC HYMN TO DEMETER
ACCOUNT OF THE CARRYING AWAY OF PERSEPHONE

I sing of the sacred goddess, radiant haired Demeter,   I
and of her fine limbed daughter whom Hades
ravished, having received her as a gift from Zeus, whose
    stroke is heavy, whose view is long.
He led her far from Demeter of the golden scimitar,
    of the sweet fruits,
while she played with the deep bosomed daughters of Ocean,
gathering flowers: roses and crocuses and beautiful violets,
in a soft grassy meadow, with iris and hyacinth.

[1] From *Les Intuitions Préchrétiennes*, pages 9-21.
[2] Faint and weary thou hast sought me.

I

And narcissus also, which was brought forth as a snare for
    the maiden with the rosebud face
By Earth, showing favour, according to the will of Zeus, to him
    who gathers all.
And she made it bright and marvellous; all were awed at the sight,
Out of its root a hundred flowers sprang up;
It gave off a lovely scent, and the whole broad heaven above
and all the earth smiled, and the salt swell of the sea.
She began to tremble, and stretched out both her hands,
to seize the beautiful toy. Then the earth with its wide paths
    gaped open
over the Nysian plain; there the king arose, he who harvests,
with his immortal horses, Kronos's son of many names.
He caught her up against her will into his golden chariot.
He carried her, weeping and crying at the top of her voice,
invoking her father, Kronos's son, supreme and perfect, god. . . .
In spite of herself he took her away by the counsel of Zeus
He the brother of her father, who commands,   30
    and who gathers all.

(The grief of Demeter hinders the growing of the wheat; the
human species would have perished and the gods been without
honour, if Zeus had not sent word to Hades that he must allow
the maiden to depart. Hades listens to the message: smiling. And
he says to her:)

'Go, Persephone, home to your mother of the blue veil   360
Since in your breast you have the courage and the heart
    of a child
And do not torment yourself so much too much,
For among the immortals I am a bridegroom not without
    honour.
I, own brother of your father Zeus. Dwelling here below, I,
You would rule over all that lives, and all that moves,
And among the immortals you would have the highest
    honours.'

Thus he spoke. The prudent Persephone was delighted   370
Immediately she started up with joy. She arose
and he gave her a pomegranate seed, sweet as honey, to
    eat in secret
planning for her, that she might not remain for always
there above with the reverend Demeter of the blue veil.

(Henceforth she passes two-thirds of the year with her mother, among the gods, and one-third with Hades.)

Hades or Aïdoneus, a name which means Invisible or Eternal, or the two at once, is presented sometimes as the brother of Zeus, sometimes as Zeus himself; for there is a subterranean Zeus. The name of Demeter very probably means Earth-mother, and Demeter is identical with all those goddess mothers whose cult has so many analogies with the role played by the Virgin in the Catholic conception. The narcissus flower represents Narcissus, a being so beautiful that he could be in love only with himself. The only beauty which can be an object of love for itself, which can be its own object, is the divine beauty. The soul in quest of pleasure encounters the divine beauty which appears here below in the form of the beauty of the world, as a snare for the soul. By the power of this snare, God seizes the soul in spite of itself. This is the very same conception that we find in Plato's *Phaedrus*. God must allow the soul to return to nature; but before that, by surprise and by strategy, He furtively gives it a pomegranate seed to eat. If the soul eats this, it is captured for ever. The pomegranate seed is that consent which the soul gives to God almost without knowing it, and without admitting it to itself. This is as an infinitely small thing among all the carnal inclinations of the soul, and nevertheless this decides its destiny for ever. This is the grain of mustard seed to which Christ compares the Kingdom of Heaven, the smallest of the seeds, but which later shall become that tree wherein the birds of heaven alight.

There are in this myth two successive acts of violence to which God subjects the soul, one which is pure violence, another to which the soul's consent to God is indispensable and upon which its salvation depends. These two moments are found also in the myth of the *Phaedrus* and in that of the Cave. They have an analogy in the parable in the Gospels concerning the wedding banquet, for which servants go into the highways to seek guests at random among those who happen to be there, but for which only those are retained who have on the wedding garment. They have an analogy in the opposition between the 'called' and the 'Elect', and also in the parable of the virgins who go out together to find the bridegroom but among whom only those who have oil in their lamps are admitted, etc.

The idea of a snare set for man by God is also the meaning of the myth of the labyrinth, if one takes away the stories added afterwards which refer to the wars between Crete and Athens. Minos, son of Zeus, judge of the dead, is that unique being whose names in antiquity are Osiris, Dionysus, Prometheus, Love, Hermes, Apollo and many others. (The credibility of these assimilations can be established.) The Minotaur is the same being represented as the bull, just as Osiris is represented under the form of the Ox Apis and Dionysus–Zagreus with horns (a symbolism which relates to the moon and to its phases may explain this image). The labyrinth is that path where man, from the moment he enters upon it, loses his way and finds himself equally powerless, at the end of a certain time, to return upon his steps or to direct himself anywhere. He errs without knowing where, and finally arrives at the place where God waits to devour him.

*　　*　　*

SCOTCH TALE OF THE DUKE OF NORWAY

(This story is repeated in the folklore of Russia, Germany, et cetera.)

A prince (here called 'the Duke o' Norroway') has, during the day, the form of an animal and at night only, a human form. A princess marries him. One night, tired of this situation, she destroys her husband's animal hide. But then he disappears. She must search for him.

She searches endlessly, walking across the plains and the forests. In the course of her wanderings, she meets an old woman who makes her a present of three marvellous nuts to be used in case of distress. On and on she wanders for a very long time. At last she finds a palace where the prince lives, her husband in his human form. But he has forgotten her and in a few days he is going to take another wife. The princess, after her interminable journey, is in a miserable state, in rags. She enters the palace as a kitchen maid. She breaks one of the nuts, finds in it a wonderful gown. She offers this gown to the fiancée in exchange for the privilege of passing one whole night with the prince. The fiancée hesitates, then, tempted by the gown, accepts; but first she makes the prince take a drug which keeps him asleep the whole night. While he sleeps, the kitchen maid, who is his true wife, is at his side and without ceasing she sings:

'Far hae I sought ye, near am I brought to ye;
Dear Duke o' Norroway, will ye turn and speak to me?'

She sings *till her heart was like to break, and over again to break.*

He does not awake and at dawn she has to leave him. A second night the same thing happens and still a third. Then, just before dawn the prince awakes, he recognizes his true wife and sends the other away.

This story also represents, in my opinion, the quest of man by God. It contains, moreover, the two moments of God's capture of man. The first takes place in the night of the unconscious, while man's consciousness is still entirely instinctive and his humanity is hidden within him; as soon as God would draw him into the light, man flees, disappears far from God, forgets Him, and prepares for an adulterous union with the flesh. God seeks man with pain and fatigue and reaches him as a beggar. God entices the flesh by means of beauty and obtains access to the soul but finds it sleeping. A term of delay in which to awaken is accorded the soul. If only it wakes an instant before the expiration of this delay, recognizes God, and chooses Him, then the soul is saved. The fact that the prince awakens only one minute before the third and last dawn signifies that at the decisive moment the difference between the soul which is saved and that which is lost is but infinitesimal compared with the whole psychological content of the soul. It is this also which is meant in the Gospels by the likening of the Kingdom of Heaven to a grain of mustard, to leaven, to a pearl, etc., in the same way as the pomegranate seed of Persephone.

The miserable appearance of the princess, her coming into the palace as a kitchen maid, indicates that God comes to us completely bereft not only of His power, but also of His beauty and lustre. He comes to us hidden, and salvation consists in recognizing Him.

There is another theme from folklore which doubtless refers to the same truth; it is that of the princess who leaves for a long journey accompanied by a slave to marry a prince (in certain tales it is a prince who with his slave goes to marry a princess). Along the way an event forces the princess to change her clothes and her robe with that of her slave and to take a vow never to reveal her true identity. The prince prepares to marry the slave, and it is only at the last minute that he recognizes his real fiancée.

The two themes may also be regarded as evoking the Passion. In the tale of the 'Duke of Norway', the interminable walk, exhausting to the legitimate bride, which makes her arrive at the prince's palace in a sordid state, barefoot and in rags, is perfectly appropriate to this evocation. The phrase 'Far hae I sought ye, near am I brought to ye' then takes on a heart-rending signification. And also the words 'she sang till her heart was like to break, and over again to break.'

*   *   *

THE MUTUAL RECOGNITION OF GOD AND OF MAN
SOPHOCLES: ELECTRA AND ORESTES

Electra, 1218 ff.

ELECTRA: Where is the grave of that unhappy man?
ORESTES: He has none. The living have no tomb.

6

ELECTRA: What do you mean, my child?

ORESTES: There is nothing untrue in my words.

ELECTRA: Is he then a living man?

ORESTES: Yes, if breath is in me.

ELECTRA: Are you then he?

ORESTES: Examine this, my father's ring, and see if I speak the truth.

ELECTRA: O beloved light!

ORESTES: Beloved, I am its witness.

ELECTRA: O voice—are you there?

ORESTES: No longer question elsewhere.

ELECTRA: I have you in my arms?

ORESTES: Thus henceforth forever hold me.

ELECTRA: O dearest women, fellow-citizens, behold Orestes who found a means to die, now has found means to be saved.

If one reads these lines without thinking of the story of Electra and Orestes, the mystical overtones are evident. (Never again question elsewhere—thus hold me forever.) If after that one thinks of the story just as it is in Sophocles, the evidence becomes even greater.

Here it is a question of recognition, a frequent theme in folklore. One believes a stranger is before one, but it is the most loved being. This is what happened to Mary Magdalene and a certain gardener.

Electra is the daughter of a powerful king, but reduced to the most miserable state of slavery by the orders of those who have betrayed her father. She is hungry. She is in rags. Affliction not only crushes her, it degrades and embitters her. But she makes no covenant. She hates these enemies of her father who have all power over her. Only her brother, who is far away, could deliver her. She is consumed with waiting. At last he comes, but she does not recognize him. She believes she sees a stranger who announces her brother's death and brings his ashes. She falls into a bottomless despair, she hopes to die. But even though she hopes for nothing, she never for an instant thinks of giving in. She only hates her enemies the more intensely. While she holds the urn, weeping, Orestes, who had taken her for a slave, recognizes her by her tears. He informs her than the urn is empty. He reveals himself to her.

There is a double recognition. God recognizes the soul by its tears, then makes Himself known to it.

Just when the soul is spent and has ceased to wait for God, when the external affliction or the interior aridity forces it to believe that God is not a reality, if then nevertheless the soul still loves, and holds in horror those worldly riches which would take his place, then it is that God comes to the soul, reveals Himself, speaks to it, touches it. This is what St. John of the Cross names the dark night of the soul.

Furthermore, the mourning caused by the urn and the ashes of Orestes, followed by the joy of recognition, evokes as clearly as possible the theme of God who dies and is resurrected.

One verse designates this theme without ambiguity: μηχαναῖσι μὲν θανόντα, νῦν δὲ μηχαναῖς σεσωσμένον. A stratagem caused his death, now a stratagem has saved him.

But the word stratagem is not appropriate. The word μηχανή is employed, by the tragic poets, Plato, Pindar, Herodotus, in many texts which have a reference to, clear or hidden, direct or indirect, certain or conjectural, the ideas of salvation and of redemption, notably in *Prometheus*. This is made credible by the fact that the same word has been used upon the same subject in the Mysteries. This word defines itself as *means* and is synonymous with the word πόρος (concerning which see the commentary on the myth of the birth of Love in the *Symposium*). This word is employed in a text by Herodotus which refers as clearly as possible to the Passion. The corresponding Latin word is *machina*. That god, who descends upon the scene at the end of the play, is called *Deus ex machina*.

Among the Greek poets, Sophocles is the one whose quality of inspiration is the most visibly Christian and perhaps the most pure (he is to my knowledge much more Christian than any tragic poet of the last twenty centuries). This Christian quality is generally recognized in the tragedy of *Antigone*, which might be an illustration of the saying: 'We ought to obey God rather than men.' The god who presides over this tragedy is not known as being in heaven, but beneath the earth. It comes to the same thing. It is always to the true God, the God who is in the other world, that reference is made. Man in his charity must imitate the impartiality of God who watches over all. It is this that Christ bids us to imitate: the perfection of the Celestial Father who makes the rain to fall and the sun to shine over all creation.

CREON: Was he not your brother, who died fighting him? (i.e. in fighting Polynices. He refers to Eteocles).

ANTIGONE: My brother, born of one woman and of the same father. [Simone Weil translates: 'born of one and the same father.']

CREON: How then do you count as kindness what is dishonour to that other?

ANTIGONE: The dead corpse will not bear witness thus.

CREON: He will if you only honour him as much as the ungodly one—

ANTIGONE: But it was not a slave, but a brother who died.

CREON: Laying waste the land; the other was defending it.

ANTIGONE: Nevertheless the God of the Dead at least desires equality.

CREON: But not that the good should win an equal share with the bad.

ANTIGONE: Who knows if this is sacred in the world below?

CREON: Never at any time is the enemy, even when dead, a friend.

ANTIGONE: I was born not to share in hate but to share in love.

This verse spoken by Antigone is splendid; but Creon's reply is even more splendid, for it shows that those who share only in love and not in hate belong to another world and have nothing to expect from this world but a violent death.

v. 525—'Descend then, since you have such need to love, love those who are below.'

It is only among the dead, in the other world, that one is free to love. This present world does not authorize love. It is only the dead whom one may love; that is to say, the souls in so far as by destiny they belong to the other world.

Antigone is a perfectly pure being, perfectly innocent, perfectly heroic, who voluntarily gives herself up to death to preserve a guilty brother from an unhappy fate in the other world. At the moment when imminent death approaches her her nature betrays her, she feels herself abandoned by men and by the gods. She perishes for having loved beyond reason, Her sister tells her at the beginning: ἄνους μὲν ἔρχῃ, τοῖς φίλοις δ' ὀρθῶς φίλη. 'You are mad, but for your friends, a true friend.' (Line 99) Compare the *Prometheus* of Aeschylus.)

In several Greek tragedies we observe a curse born of a sin transmitted from generation to generation until it strikes a perfectly guiltless person who suffers all the bitterness of it. Then the curse is ended. Thus a curse is born of a sin of disobedience to God committed by Laios. The guiltless person who stops it by the fact that he endures it is Eteocles in Aeschylus, Antigone in Sophocles. The guiltless person who stops the curse of the Pelopids is Orestes in Aeschylus (the *Electra* of Sophocles is not in that perspective). What is called Fate in Greek tragedy has been very badly misunderstood. There is no such agency apart from this conception of the curse, which, once produced by a crime, is handed down by men from one to another and cannot be destroyed except by the suffering of a pure victim obedient to God.

II

THE LAMENTS OF ELECTRA AND
THE RECOGNITION OF ORESTES[1]

Sophocles, *Electra*, 117

ELECTRA: May God send me my brother!
    Alone I can no longer endure
    these griefs beneath which I am bowed. . . .
    Without rest I await him. Having no children   164
    alas! nor husband, I fail day by day
    and my tears endlessly flow. All vainly
    griefs pile upon griefs, still he forgets me. . . .
    The best part of my life is already past,   185
    poured out in despair. I have no more strength.
    Bereft of parents, sorrow corrodes me.
    There is no man to love or protect me.
    I must, like the least of his servants,
    work in my father's house;
    clothed in humiliating rags
    I must wait, standing by his empty tables. . . .
    In my own home, with the murderer of my father   262
    I must live: following his orders, depending upon him
    to provide my living, or to impose privations. . . .
    Under such conditions, dear friends, I cannot be either good 307

[1] From *La Source Grecque*, pages 47-56.

or reasonable. Those to whom evil is done
cannot save themselves from becoming evil. . . .

As for me, I would never submit to these people,   359
not even if anyone would give me gifts
such as you now luxuriate in. You may have
the sumptuously decked tables, the abundant life. . . .
I envy none of your privileges. . . .   364

Only let him come now as quickly as he may! . . .   389
   That I may part from among you as quickly as possible.   391
CHRY. Have you no concern to save your life?
ELEC. It is a beautiful life truly! One may well admire it!
CHRY. But you might live happily if you were reasonable.
ELEC. Counsel me no cowardice with regard to my own.
CHRY. My advice is only that you submit to those who are
   stronger. . . .

ELEC. Orestes beloved! How you destroy me by dying. . . .   808
   I am wretched. Where now can I put my trust?   811
   I am alone since I am bereft of you
   and of my father. Once again I must yield to the orders
   of my bitterest enemies. . . .
   But no, I would rather yield the time that is left me to live,
   I want no more of it. I shall sit before this door,
   friendless, waiting for my life to burn out.

If from the moment when Orestes speaks, one reads the above
dialogue with the thought that it concerns Christ and the soul,
certain thoughts become overwhelming. First one should read
almost all of Electra's laments with this understanding. In the
opening lines spoken by Orestes the word μηχανή occurs, here
I seem to recognize a liturgical term from the Mysteries of
Eleusis relating to the Redemption. Electra, whom Orestes has
not yet recognized in the guise of a slave, has succeeded in taking
in her hands the urn which is said to contain Orestes' ashes. She
proceeds to mourn for her brother. The sending away of the

child Orestes, to save him from the massacre, which Electra recalls, reminds one of the Flight into Egypt. Each word of the lines which follow have, besides their external sense, a perfectly manifest mystical sense.

ELECTRA: O vestige of him who was for me the best beloved of
    humans,   1126
    last trace of the life of Orestes, how contrary
    to my hope in sending you forth I receive you back!
    Now I weigh you in my hands and you are nothing,
    but as a child from this house I sent you forth in splendour.   1130
    If only you had been able to quit this life earlier
    before I sent you into a strange land,
    these hands that stole you away to save you from murder.
    For you would have died here in that long ago day,
    here also you would have shared in your father's tomb.   1135
    But as it is, away from home, upon foreign soil, in exile,
    you have perished miserably and your sister was not near.
    I was not able with tender hands, I, grief-stricken,
    to wash and prepare you and upon a blazing fire
    to carry you as one ought to carry such a precious burden.   1140
    No, the hands of strangers tended your misery.
    Little weight now, here in this little vessel.
    Alas, I grieve that those fond cares of long ago
    are useless now, which often and not without sweet cost,
    I lavished upon you.   For never   1145
    your own mother held you more dear than I.
    You were not brought up by servants but by myself alone.
    It was I, your sister, whom you always were calling.
    Now such things have vanished in a single day
    with you who are dead; you have swept them all away with
       you   1150
    like a tempest. He is dead, our father,
    I am dead in you, you disappeared in death.
    Our enemies mock us, she is delirious with pleasure,
    that mother who is no mother, on whom, as you often
    secretly told me, you would have returned   1155
    to take vengeance. But this, the tragedy

of our destiny, yours and mine, has forbidden
and has sent back to me thus, in place of your beloved
person, these ashes and a useless shadow.
Alas, alas.   1160
Pitiful body.
Ah, ah
how terrible it is!
I am afflicted.
On what terrible paths you were sent, and so made me lost!
You did truly lose me, O thou, my brother's head!
So now I come to you, receive me in your dwelling,   1165
that one which is not illusion, thus with you below
I may dwell henceforth. For when you were here
we shared the same fate. And how I long
for death with you and to share your tomb.
For those who are dead, I think, do not suffer.   1170
CHORUS: Your father was mortal, Electra, be moderate.
        Orestes was mortal. You must not grieve too much
for this is a debt we all have to pay.
ORESTES: Alas! Alas! What shall I say! What impossible words
        rise in me! I can no longer constrain my speech.   1175
ELECTRA: What do you suffer? To what do your words refer?
ORESTES: Is this the illustrious being, Electra, here before me?
ELECTRA: This is she, and in what a dreadful state!
ORESTES: Ah, unhappy one! Ah, what misfortune is here!
ELECTRA: It is not certainly over me, stranger, that you so
        bemoan.   1180
ORESTES: How shamefully, criminally, has this body been wasted!
ELECTRA: It is thus truly of none other than myself that you speak
        this ill, stranger.
ORESTES:Ah, this is not for a young girl, this degradation in which
        you live.
ELECTRA: What is there, stranger, in the sight of me to make you
        groan?
ORESTES: It is that I knew nothing till now of my own affliction. 1185
ELECTRA: From which of my words did you learn it?
ORESTES: By seeing you clothed in a multitude of sorrows.
ELECTRA: And yet you see but a small part of my pains.

14

ORESTES: And how could there be any more frightful to see?

ELECTRA: This: that I live among murderers. 1190

ORESTES: Murderers of whom? Who brings you to this?

ELECTRA: Of my father; moreover they have forced me to be a slave.

ORESTES: Who subjects you to this constraint, who among men?

ELECTRA: She is called my mother, but is nothing of a mother.

ORESTES: But how, by what blows or ill-treatments? 1195

ELECTRA: By blows and mistreatments and all evil ways.

ORESTES: And was there none to stand against them, none to defend you?

ELECTRA: No, certainly. He whom I had you bring back to me in ashes.

ORESTES: Poor sufferer, what pity I have felt since I first saw you.

ELECTRA: Know this, that you are the only being who has ever pitied me. 1200

ORESTES: That is because I alone am here to grieve for your sufferings.

ELECTRA: Might you perhaps be in some way related to us?

ORESTES: I would explain this to you if these women were loyal.

ELECTRA: They are loyal, you may speak in confidence.

ORESTES: First, that you may learn all, relinquish this urn. 1205

ELECTRA: No, in the name of the Gods, stranger, do not force me to this.

ORESTES: Trust in my word and you will do well.

ELECTRA: No, I solemnly beg you not to take from me all that I love.

ORESTES: I will not let go.

ELECTRA: How afflicted am I for your sake, Orestes, if I must be deprived of your sepulchre! . . . 1210

ORESTES: It is not fitting that you should hold it.[1] 1213

ELECTRA: Am I then to such degree unworthy of him who is dead?

ORESTES: You are unworthy of no one. But this does not belong to you.

ELECTRA: Why not, since it is the body of Orestes which I hold here?

ORESTES: But this is not the body of Orestes, or only by trickery.

ELECTRA: Then he, unhappy one, where shall I find his grave?

ORESTES: He has none. The living have no grave.

---

[1] I reconstruct this line from memory, not having my papers (Simone Weil's note).

ELECTRA: What do you say, my child?

ORESTES: There is nothing untrue in my words.   1220

ELECTRA: Is he then a living man?

ORESTES: Yes, as life is in me.

ELECTRA: Then you, you are he?

ORESTES: First only examine this ring from my father and decide
    if I speak the truth.

ELECTRA: O well-beloved light!

ORESTES: Well-beloved; I am witness to it.

ELECTRA: O voice, you are here?

ORESTES: Henceforth never doubt.   1225

ELECTRA: I hold you in my arms?

ORESTES: Thus hold me forever.

ELECTRA: O dearest women, fellow citizens,
    behold Orestes is here, he who knew the way
    to die, now finds the way to be saved.

If one accepts that Electra is the human soul exiled upon earth,
fallen into affliction and that Orestes is the Christ, how poignant
then do the words of Orestes become: 'What impossible words
rise in me! I can no longer hold back my speech.' And: 'Ah! this
is not for a young girl, this misery in which you live.' (The young
girl being the classic symbol of the soul.) And: 'Till now I knew
nothing of my own misfortunes.' And these rejoinders: 'Is there
no one to defend you, none to take your part?' 'No assuredly; you
have brought me the ashes of him whom I had.' And when
Electra says 'Know this, you are the only being who has ever
shown me pity.' The reply: 'It is that I am the only one to share
your sorrow' and 'the living have no tomb'. And: 'No falsehood
in my words.' And : 'Judge whether my word is true.' And the
sublime dialogue in three lines where Electra marvels at the
presence of her beloved with three senses successively: sight,
hearing and touch. The rejoinders of Orestes: 'Beloved, I am
witness to it'; 'Henceforth have me always?' are without meaning,
unless spoken by God. And Electra's words, 'who found means
to be dead, has found means to be saved' (once again the word
μηχανή), are clear evidence.

Electra is obliged to stretch her detachment to its extreme limit, even to do violence to her love for Orestes, before Orestes reveals himself to her. She must let go the urn.

Before Orestes begins to speak, when Electra believes that nothing exists of all that she holds dear, that in the world are only her enemies, who are at the same time her masters, she never for an instant dreams of trying to pacify or conciliate them. Her only thought is that since he whom she loves is in oblivion, she must also, by death, enter oblivion, she who is still alive feels herself already in oblivion. Belief in the apparently certain evidence that he whom she loves is absolutely non-existent never diminishes her love, but on the contrary increases it. This is the sort of fidelity raised to the point of madness which compels Orestes to reveal himself. He can no longer restrain himself from it; he is over-powered by compassion.

III

ANTIGONE[1]

EDITOR'S NOTE

THE ARTICLE entitled 'Antigone' was published before the war in a little factory magazine: *Between Ourselves, Chronicle of Rosieres* (May 16th, 1936). It was found again recently by M. Jacques Caband at Rosieres, near Bourges. A letter published in *La Condition Ouvrière* (pp. 153-4) which Simone Weil wrote in April or May 1936 to the director of the factory, who was also editor of the magazine, shows the character of this work and her intention in writing it.

'I wondered, anxiously, how I could take upon myself to write within the required limits, for obviously it was a question of giving you the most appropriate prose of which I am capable. Luckily I remembered an old project which is very close to my heart; that of making the masterpieces of Greek poetry (which I passionately love) available to the masses. Since last year I have felt that great Greek poetry would be a hundred times closer to the people, if it could be known by them, than classical or modern French literature could ever be. I have begun with 'Antigone'. If I have succeeded in my intention for this work, it ought to interest and touch everyone from the factory director down to the humblest employee, it ought to provide them all with complete access without the least impression of condescension or of any

[1] From *La Source Grecque*, pages 57-63.

arrangements having been made to bring the work within their reach. It is thus that I understand popularization. But I don't know whether I have succeeded.

*　　*　　*

Almost two thousand five hundred years ago in Greece, some very beautiful poems were written. These are hardly read any more except by people who specialize in the subject; and this is a very great pity, because these old poems are so truly human that they are still very close to us and can interest everyone. In fact, they would be much more moving for ordinary people, who know what it is to struggle and to suffer, than for those who have spent their lives between the four walls of a library.

Sophocles is one of the greatest among these old poets. He has written works for the theatre, dramas and comedies; only a few of his dramas have come down to us. In each one of these the principal character is a courageous and noble being who wrestles alone against an intolerably painful situation; he is bowed down by the weight of solitude, of humiliation, of poverty, of injustice; at times his courage is at the breaking point, but he holds on and never lets himself be corrupted by misfortune. For that reason, no matter how painful they are, these dramas never leave us with an impression of sadness. Instead, they leave an impression of serenity.

Antigone is the title of one of these dramas. It is the story of a human being who, all alone, without any backing, dares to be in opposition to her own country, to the laws of that country, to the head of its government, and who is, naturally, soon put to death.

This takes place in a Greek city named Thebes. Two brothers, after the death of their father, are rivals for his throne, one of them succeeds in exiling the other and he becomes king. The exiled brother finds backing abroad; he returns with a foreign army to attack his native land in the hope of regaining power. There is a battle; the foreigners are put to flight; but the two brothers come face to face on the battlefield, and there they kill each other.

Their uncle becomes king. He decides that the two bodies shall not be treated in the same manner. One of the brothers died defending his country; his body shall be buried with all the conventional honours. The other died in attacking his country; his body shall be abandoned, left to rot on the ground, the prey of crows and wild animals. Here it is important to know that for the Greeks there could never be a greater shame or dishonour than to be treated in this way after death. The king let the citizens know his decision and at the same time let them know that whoever tried to bury the dishonoured corpse would be killed.

The dead brothers left two sisters who are still young girls. One of them, Ismene, is just a shy, sweet girl such as you see anywhere; the other, Antigone, has a loving heart and heroic courage. She cannot endure the thought that her brother's body will be treated so shamefully. Between two loyalties, the loyalty to her vanquished brother and the loyalty to her victorious country, she does not hesitate an instant. She refuses to abandon her brother, this brother whose memory is defiled by the people and by the State. She decides to bury his body despite the king's command and his threat of death.

The play begins with a dialogue between Antigone and her sister Ismene. Antigone wants Ismene to help her. Ismene is terrified; her disposition is better adapted for obedience than for revolt.

> We must submit ourselves to those who are strongest 63
> Execute all their orders, even more painful ones. . . .
> For myself I shall obey those in power 67
> I was not made to stand up against the State.

In Antigone's eyes this submission is cowardice. She will act alone.

Meanwhile the citizens of Thebes, rejoicing for the victory and the re-establishment of peace, celebrate the dawn of a new order:

> Shaft of the rising sun 100
> You bring to Thebes the fairest light

Antigone

You appear at last
O golden eye of day.

It is no sooner discovered that someone has attempted to bury
the dishonoured body than Antigone is caught in the act, and she
is brought before the king. For him the whole affair is first of all
a question of authority. The order of the State requires that the
authority of its chief be respected. He sees in what Antigone has
done an act of disobedience to the country. That is why he speaks
to her harshly. As for her, she denies nothing. She knows she is
lost. Yet she does not waver for an instant.

Thy orders, to my mind, have less authority   453
than the unwritten and inscrutable laws of God.
All these present here approve me,   504
they would declare it if fear had not closed their mouths.
But rulers possess many privileges, and above all
that to act and to speak as they please.

A dialogue between them ensues. He judges everything from
the point of view of the State; she holds to another view which
seems to her superior. He recalls that the two brothers did not
die under the same conditions:

THE KING: One was attacking his country, the other defending it.
     Should the loyal man and the traitor be treated alike?
ANTIGONE: Who knows what value these distinctions have among
     the dead?
THE KING: An enemy, even when he is dead, does not become a
     friend.
ANTIGONE: I was born not to share in hate, but only in love.

Ismene arrives; now she wants to share in her sister's fate, to die
with her. Antigone will not permit this but tries to calm her:

You have chosen to live, I to die.   555
Take courage and live. As for me, my soul is already dead.   559

The king has the two young girls led away. But his son, who is
engaged to Antigone, tries to intercede for her whom he loves.
The king only sees in this attempt a new threat to his authority.

21

He goes into a violent rage, especially when the young man dares to say that the people pity Antigone. At this point the argument turns to a quarrel. The king cries out:

THE KING: Is it not for me alone to rule this country? 734
THE KING'S SON: There is no city which should belong to a single man.
KING: Then does not the land belong to the ruler?
SON: You may as well, in that case, rule alone in a deserted land.

The king holds on, the young man is beside himself, but gains nothing and leaves in despair. A few citizens of Thebes who have witnessed the quarrel, admire the power of love.

> Love, invincible in combat, 781
> Love, stealing into houses
> and coming to rest
> upon the soft cheeks of young girls;
> You range beyond the seas,
> and enter the peasant's stable,
> none escapes you, either among the immortal gods
> or among men who live but a day.
> And whoever loves is mad.

At this moment Antigone appears, led by the king. He, holding both her hands, drags her to her doom. She is not to be killed, for the Greeks believed it was unlucky to take the life of a young girl; but they do worse. She is to be buried alive. She is to be thrust into a cave and the cave walled up so that she may agonize there slowly, in the darkness, starving and asphyxiated. Only a few instants are left to her. She stands at the very threshold of death, and of a death so atrocious that the pride which supported her breaks. She weeps.

> Turn your eyes toward me, citizens of my country. 806
> I follow my last course.
> I see the last rays of the setting sun,
> I shall never see any others.

She hears no comforting word. Those who surround her are careful, in the king's presence, to deny her the least sign of sympathy; they are satisfied to remind her coldly that she would have done better not to have disobeyed. The king in the most brutal tone gives her the order to hurry. But she still cannot resign herself to silence.

> See how I am by both hands dragged forth 916
> I, a virgin, without husband; I who have not had my share
> either of marriage, or of nourishing children.
> Abandoned as I am and unfriended, alas!
> I shall enter still living into the grave of the dead.
> What crime have I committed before God?
> Why must I, unhappy one, still turn my eyes
> toward God, Whom may I call to my aid? Ah!
> It is for having done what is right that so much wrong is done me.
> But if before God my affliction is legitimate,
> then in the midst of my suffering I will recognize my fault.
> But if it is they who are at fault, I shall not wish them
> more sorrows than they make me suffer unjustly.

The king loses patience and ends by carrying her off by force. He returns after sealing the cave where he has thrust her. But it is his turn now to suffer. A priest who can tell the future predicts the most terrible disasters for him if he does not deliver Antigone. After a long and violent discussion the king gives in. The cave is opened and there Antigone is found already dead, having succeeded in strangling herself. There also her fiancé is found, convulsively kissing her corpse. The young man had chosen to be entombed with her. As soon as he sees his father he gets up and in an excess of frustrated fury, kills himself before his father's eyes. The queen, as she learns of her son's suicide, kills herself also. When news of her death is announced to the king, this man who knew so well how to speak as a master breaks down, mastered by sorrow. And the citizens of Thebes conclude:

> The haughty words of arrogant men are paid for by terrible
>   disasters, 1350
> From which in old age they learn moderation.

IV

THE 'ILIAD', POEM OF MIGHT[1]
Homer

THE TRUE HERO, the real subject, the core of the
Iliad, is might. That which is wielded by men rules
over them, and before it man's flesh cringes. The human
soul never ceases to be modified by its encounter with might,
swept on, blinded by that which it believes itself able to handle,
bowed beneath the power of that which it suffers. Those who
dreamt that might, thanks to progress, belonged henceforth to
the past, have been able to see its living witness in this poem:
those who know how to recognize it throughout the ages, there
at the heart of every human testament, find here its most beautiful,
most pure of mirrors.

Might is that which makes a thing of anybody who comes
under its sway. When exercised to the full, it makes a thing of
man in the most literal sense, for it makes him a corpse. There
where someone stood a moment ago, stands no one. This is the
spectacle which the *Iliad* never tires of presenting.

> . . . the horses
> Thundered the empty chariots over the battle-lanes
> Mourning their noble masters. But they upon earth
> Now stretched, are dearer to vultures
>   than to their wives.

[1] From *La Source Grecque*, pages 9-43.

24

The 'Iliad', Poem of Might

The hero is become a thing dragged in the dust behind a chariot.

> All about the dark hair
> Was strewn; and the whole head lay in dust,
> That head but lately so beloved. Now Zeus had
>   permitted
> His enemies to defile it upon its native soil.

The bitterness of this scene, we savour it whole, alleviated by no comforting fiction, no consoling immortality, no faint halo of patriotic glory.

> His soul from his body took flight and sped towards
>   Hades
> Weeping over its destiny, leaving its vigour and
>   its youth.

More poignant still for its pain of contrast is the sudden evocation, as quickly effaced, of another world, the far-off world, precarious and touching of peace, of the family, that world wherein each man is, for those who surround him, all that matters most.

> Her voice rang through the house calling her
>   bright-haired maids
> To draw a great tripod to the fire that there might be
> A hot bath for Hector upon his return from combat.
> Foolish one! She knew not how far from hot baths
> The arm of Achilles had felled him because of green-
>   eyed Athena.

Indeed he was far from hot baths, this sufferer. He was not the only one. Nearly all the *Iliad* takes place far from hot baths. Nearly all of human life has always passed far from hot baths.

The might which kills outright is an elementary and coarse form of might. How much more varied in its devices; how much more astonishing in its effects is that other which does not kill; or which delays killing. It must surely kill, or it will perhaps kill, or else it is only suspended above him whom it may at any moment destroy. This of all procedures turns a man to stone.

From the power to transform him into a thing by killing him there proceeds another power, and much more prodigious, that which makes a thing of him while he still lives. He is living, he has a soul, yet he is a thing. A strange being is that thing which has a soul, and strange the state of that soul. Who knows how often during each instant it must torture and destroy itself in order to comform? The soul was not made to dwell in a thing; and when forced to it, there is no part of that soul but suffers violence.

A man naked and disarmed upon whom a weapon is directed becomes a corpse before he is touched. Only for one moment still he deliberates, he strives, he hopes.

> Motionless Achilles considered. The other drew near, seized
> By desire to touch his knees. He wished in his heart
> To escape evil death, and black destiny. . . .
> With one arm he encircled those knees to implore him,
> With the other he kept hold of his bright lance.

But soon he has understood that the weapon will not turn from him, and though he still breathes, he is only matter, still thinking, he can think of nothing.

> Thus spake the brilliant son of Priam
> With suppliant words. He hears an inflexible reply . . .
> He spoke; and the other's knees and heart failed him,
> He dropped his lance and sank to the ground with open hands,
> With both hands outstretched. Achilles unsheathes his sharp sword,
> Struck to the breastbone, along the throat, and then the two-edged sword
> Plunges home its full length. The other, face down upon the ground,
> Lay inert, his dark blood flowed drenching the earth.

When, a stranger, completely disabled, weak and disarmed, appeals to a warrior, he is not by this act condemned to death;

but only an instant of impatience on the part of the warrior suffices to deprive him of life. This is enough to make his flesh lose that principal property of all living tissue. A morsel of living flesh gives evidence of life first of all by reflex, as a frog's leg under electric shock jumps, as the approaching menace or the contact with a horrible thing, or terrifying event, provokes a shudder in no matter what bundle of flesh, nerves and muscles. Alone, the hopeless suppliant does not shudder, does not cringe; he no longer has such licence; his lips are about to touch that one of all objects which is for him the most charged with horror.

> None saw the entrance of great Priam. He paused,
> Encircled Achilles' knees, kissed those hands,
> Terrible slayers of men, that had cost him so many sons.

The spectacle of a man reduced to such a degree of misery freezes almost as does the sight of a corpse.

> As when dire misfortune strikes a man, if in his own
>   country
> He has killed, and he arrives at another's door,
> That of some wealthy man; a chill seizes those who
>   see him;
> So Achilles shivered at the sight of divine Priam,
> So those with him trembled, looking from one to the other.

But this only for a moment, soon the very presence of the sufferer is forgotten:

> He speaks. Achilles, reminded of his own father, longed to
>   weep for him.
> Taking the old man by the arm, he thrusts him
>   gently away.
> Both were lost in remembrance; the one of Hector,
>   slayer of men,
> And in tears he faints to the ground at Achilles feet.
> But Achilles wept for his father and then also
> For Patroclus. And the sound of their sobbing rocked
>   the halls.

It is not for want of sensibility that Achilles had, by a sudden gesture, pushed the old man glued against his knees to the ground. Priam's words, evoking his old father, had moved him to tears. Quite simply he had found himself to be as free in his attitudes, in his movements, as if in place of a suppliant an inert object were there touching his knees. The human beings around us exert just by their presence a power which belongs uniquely to themselves to stop, to diminish, or modify, each movement which our bodies design. A person who crosses our path does not turn aside our steps in the same manner as a street sign, no one stands up, or moves about, or sits down again in quite the same fashion when he is alone in a room as when he has a visitor. But this undefinable influence of the human presence is not exercised by those men whom a movement of impatience could deprive of their lives even before a thought had had the time to condemn them. Before these men others behave as if they were not there; and they, in turn, finding themselves in danger of being in an instant reduced to nothing, imitate nothingness. Pushed, they fall; fallen, they remain on the ground, so long as no one happens to think of lifting them up. But even if at last lifted up, honoured by cordial words, they still cannot bring themselves to take this resurrection seriously enough to dare to express a desire; an irritated tone of voice would immediately reduce them again to silence.

He spoke and the old man trembled and obeyed.

At least some suppliants, once exonerated, become again as other men. But there are others, more miserable beings, who without dying have become things for the rest of their lives. In their days is no give and take, no open field, no free road over which anything can pass to or from them. These are not men living harder lives than others, not placed lower socially than others, these are another species, a compromise between a man and a corpse. That a human being should be a thing is, from the point of view of logic, a contradiction; but when the impossible has become a reality, that contradiction is as a rent in the soul.

That thing aspires every moment to become a man, a woman, and never at any moment succeeds. This is a death drawn out the length of a life, a life that death has frozen long before extinguishing it.

A virgin, the daughter of a priest, suffers this fate:

> I will not release her. Before that old age shall
>   have taken her,
> In our dwelling, in Argos, far from her native land
> Tending the loom, and sharing my bed.

The young wife, the young mother, the wife of a prince suffers it:

> And perhaps one day in Argos you will weave cloth
>   for another
> And you shall fetch Messeian or Hyperian
>   water
> In spite of yourself, under stress of dire necessity.

The child heir to a royal sceptre suffers it:

> These doubtless shall depart in the depths of
>   hollow ships
> I among them; you, my child, will either go with me
> To a land where humiliating tasks await you
> And you will labour beneath the eyes of a pitiless master. . . .

Such a fate for her child is more frightful to the mother than death itself, the husband wishes to perish before seeing his wife reduced to it. A father calls down all the scourges of heaven upon the army that would subject his daughter to it. But for those upon whom it has fallen, so brutal a destiny wipes out damnations, revolts, comparisons, meditations upon the future and the past, almost memory itself. It does not belong to the slave to be faithful to his city or to his dead.

It is when one of those who made him lose all, who sacked his city, massacred his own under his very eyes, when one of those suffers, then the slave weeps. And why not? Only then are tears permitted him. They are even imposed. But during his servitude are not those tears always ready to flow as soon as, with impunity, they may?

> She speaks in weeping, and the women moan
> Taking Patroclus as pretext for each one's private
> anguish.

On no occasion has the slave a right to express anything if not that which may please the master. This is why, if in so barren a life, a capacity to love should be born, this love could only be for the master. Every other way is barred to the gift of loving, just as for a horse hitched to a wagon, the reins and the bridle bar all directions but one. And if by miracle there should appear the hope of becoming again someone, to what pitch would not that gratitude and that love soar for those very men who must still, because of the recent past, inspire horror?

> My husband, to whom my father and revered mother gave me,
> I saw before the city, transfixed by the sharp bronze.
> My three brothers, born of our one mother,
> So beloved! have met their fatal day.
> But you, when swift Achilles killed my husband
> And laid waste the city of divine Mynes,
> Did not allow me to weep. You promised me that the divine
> Achilles
> Would take me for his legitimate wife and carry
> me off in his vessels
> To Phthia to celebrate our marriage among the
> Myrmidons.
> Therefore without ceasing I weep for you who have
> always been so gentle.

One cannot lose more than the slave loses; he loses all inner life. He only retrieves a little if there should arise an opportunity to change his destiny. Such is the empire of might; it extends as far as the empire of nature. Nature also, where vital needs are in play, wipes out all interior life, even to a mother's sorrow.

For even Niobe of the beautiful hair had thought
 of eating,
She who saw twelve children of her house perish,
Six daughters and six sons in the flower of youth.
The sons Apollo killed with his silver bow
In his anger against Niobe; the daughters, Artemis,
 lover of arrows, slew.
It was because Niobe made herself equal to Leto saying:
'She has two children, I have given birth to many.'
And those two, although only two, brought death to all.
Nine days they lay dead; and none came to bury them.
The neighbours had become stones by the will of Zeus.
On the tenth day they were interred by the Gods of
 the sky,
But Niobe had thought of eating, when she was weary
 of tears.

None ever expressed with so much bitterness the misery of man, which renders him incapable of feeling his misery.

Might suffered at the hands of another is as much a tyranny over the soul as extreme hunger at the moment when food means life or death. And its empire is as cold, and as hard as though exercised by lifeless matter. The man who finds himself everywhere the most feeble of his fellows is as lonely in the heart of a city, or more lonely, than anyone can be who is lost in the midst of a desert.

Two cauldrons stand at the doorsill of Zeus
Wherein are the gifts he bestows, the evil in one,
 the good in the other. . . .
The man to whom he makes evil gifts he exposes to outrage;
A dreadful need pursues him across divine earth;
He wanders respected neither by men nor by Gods.

And as pitilessly as might crushes, so pitilessly it maddens whoever possesses, or believes he possesses it. None can ever truly possess it. The human race is not divided, in the *Iliad*, between the vanquished, the slaves, the suppliants on the one hand, and conquerors and masters on the other. No single man is to be found in it who is not, at some time, forced to bow beneath might. The soldiers, although free and well-armed, suffer no less outrage.

> Every man of the people whom he saw he shouted at
> And struck with his sceptre and reprimanded thus:
> 'Miserable one, be still, listen while others speak,
> Your superiors. You have neither courage nor strength,
> You count for nothing in battle, for nothing in the
>   assembly.'

Thersites pays dear for these words, though perfectly reasonable and not unlike those pronounced by Achilles:

> He strikes him so that he collapses with tears fast flowing,
> A bloody welt rises upon his back
> Beneath the golden sceptre; he sits down, frightened.
> In a stupor of pain he wipes his tears.
> The others, though troubled, found pleasure and
>   laughed.

But even Achilles, that proud unvanquished hero, is shown to us at the beginning of the poem weeping for humiliation and frustrating pain after the woman he had wanted for his wife was carried away under his very eyes and without his having dared to offer any opposition.

> . . . But Achilles,
> Weeping, sat down at a distance far from his companions,
> Beside the whitening waves, his eyes fixed upon
>   the boundless sea.

Agamemnon humiliates Achilles deliberately to show that he is the master.

> . . . Thus you will realize
> That I have more power than you, and all others shall tremble
> To treat me as an equal and to contradict me.

But a few days later even the supreme leader weeps in his turn, is forced to humble himself, to plead and to know the sorrow of doing so in vain.

Neither is the shame of fear spared to a single one of the combatants. The heroes tremble with the others. A challenge from Hector suffices to throw into consternation all the Greeks without the least exception, except Achilles and his men, who are absent.

> He speaks and all were silent and held their peace;
> They were ashamed to refuse, frightened to accept.

But from the moment that Ajax advances, fear changes sides:

> The Trojans felt a shiver of terror through their limbs,
> Even Hector's heart bounded in his breast,
> But he no longer had licence to tremble or
>   seek refuge.

Two days later, it is Ajax's turn to feel terror:

> Zeus, the father, from above causes fear to mount
>   in Ajax;
> He stands, distraught, putting his seven-skinned
>   shield behind him,
> Trembling before the crowd like a beast at bay.

It happens once, even to Achilles: he trembles and groans with fright, not, it is true, before a man but before a great river. Himself excepted, absolutely all are at some moment shown vanquished. Valour contributes less in determining victory than blind destiny, which is represented by the golden scales of Zeus:

> At this moment Zeus the father makes use of his
>   golden scales.
> Placing therein the two fates of death that reaps all,
> One for the Trojans, breakers of horses, one for the
>   bronze-clad Greeks.
> He seized the scales in the middle; it was the fatal day of the
>   Greeks that sank.

Because it is blind, destiny establishes a sort of justice, blind also, which punishes men of arms with death by the sword; the *Iliad* formulated the justice of retaliation long before the Gosepls, and almost in the same terms:

Ares is equitable, he kills those who kill.

If all men, by the act of being born, are destined to suffer violence, that is a truth to which the empire of circumstances closes their minds. The strong man is never absolutely strong, nor the weak man absolutely weak, but each one is ignorant of this. They do not believe that they are of the same species. The weak man no more regards himself as like the strong man than he is regarded as such. He who possesses strength moves in an atmosphere which offers him no resistance. Nothing in the human element surrounding him is of a nature to induce, between the intention and the act, that brief interval where thought may lodge. Where there is no room for thought, there is no room either for justice or prudence. This is the reason why men of arms behave with such harshness and folly. Their weapon sinks into an enemy disarmed at their knees; they triumph over a dying man, describing to him the outrages that his body will suffer; Achilles beheads twelve Trojan adolescents on Patroclus' funeral pyre as naturally as we cut flowers for a tomb. They never guess as they exercise their power, that the consequences of their acts will turn back upon themselves. When with a word one can make an old man be silent, obey, tremble, does one reflect upon the importance in the eyes of the gods of the curses of the old man, who is also a priest? Does one abstain from carrying off the woman Achilles loves when one knows she and he cannot do otherwise than obey? While Achilles enjoys the sight of the unhappy Greeks in flight, can he think that this flight, which will last as long and finish when he wills, may cost the life of his friend and even his own life? Thus it is that those to whom destiny lends might, perish for having relied too much upon it.

It is impossible that they should not perish. For they never think of their own strength as a limited quanity, nor of their relations with others as an equilibrium of unequal powers. Other men do not impose upon their acts that moment for pausing from which alone our consideration for our fellows proceeds: they conclude from this that destiny has given all licence to them and none to their inferiors. Henceforth they go beyond the measure of their strength, inevitably so, because they do not know its limit. Thus they are delivered up helpless before chance, and things no longer obey them. Sometimes chance serves them, at other times it hinders, and here they are, exposed, naked before misfortune without that armour of might which protected their souls, without anything any more to separate them from tears.

This retribution, of a geometric strictness, which punishes automatically the abuse of strength, became the principal subject of meditation for the Greeks. It constitutes the soul of the Greek epic; under the name of Nemesis it is the mainspring of Aeschylus' tragedies. The Pythagoreans, Socrates, Plato, take this as the point of departure for their thoughts about man and the universe. The notion has become familiar wherever Hellenism has penetrated. It is perhaps this Greek idea which subsists, under the name of Kharma, in Oriental countries impregnated by Buddhism; but the Occident has lost it and has not even in any one of its languages a word to express it; the ideas of limit, of measure, of equilibrium, which should determine the conduct of life, have no more than a servile usage in its technique. We are only geometricians in regard to matter; the Greeks were first of all geometricians in the apprenticeship of virtue.

The progress of the war in the *Iliad* is no more than this play of the scales. The victor of the moment feels himself invincible, even when only a few hours earlier he had experienced defeat; he forgets to partake of victory as of a thing which must pass. At the end of the first day of combat recounted in the *Iliad*, the victorious Greeks could doubtless have obtained the object of their efforts, that is, Helen and her wealth; at least if one supposes, as Homer does, that the Greek army was right to believe that Helen was in Troy. The Egyptian priests, however, who ought to have known, affirmed later to Herodotus that she was in Egypt.

In any case, on that particular evening, the Greeks did not want her.

> 'Let us at present accept neither the wealth of Paris
> Nor of Helen; each one sees, even the most ignorant,
> That Troy now stands at the edge of doom.'
> He spoke and all among the Achaeans acclaimed.

What they want is no less than all. All the riches of Troy as booty, all the palaces, the temples and the houses as ashes, all the women and all the children as slaves, all the men as corpses. They forget one detail; this is that all is not in their power; for they are not in Troy. Perhaps they may be there tomorrow, perhaps never.

Hector, that very day, succumbs to the same fault of memory:

> For this I know well in my entrails and in my heart;
> That day will come when holy Ilion shall perish
> And Priam of the mighty sword and Priam's nation.
> But I think less of the sorrow prepared for the Trojans,
> Less of Hecuba herself, and of King Priam,
> And my brothers, so many and so brave,
> Who will fall to the dust beneath the enemy's lash,
> Than of you, when one of the Greeks in bronze
>   armour
> Shall drag you away weeping, and rob you of your liberty.
> For myself: may I be dead and may the earth cover me
> Before I hear your cries or see you dragged away.

What would he not give at this moment to avoid such horrors which he believes inevitable? All that he can offer must be in vain. Yet only two days later the Greeks fled miserably, and Agamemnon himself wanted to take to the sea again. Hector, who by giving way a little might easily have obtained the enemy's departure, was no longer willing to allow them to leave with empty hands:

> Let us build fires everywhere that their brilliance
>   may enflame the sky
> For fear lest into the darkness the long-haired Greeks

> May flee away and throw themselves upon the broad
>   back of the seas. . . .
> Let more than one carry a wound to digest even at
>   home,
> And thus may all the world be afraid
> To bring to the Trojans, tamers of horses, the
>   misery of war.

His desire is carried out, the Greeks remain, and the next day, at noon, they make a pitiable object of Hector and his forces.

> They, fleeing across the plain, were like cattle
> Which a lion coming in the night drives before him. . . .
> Thus the mighty Agamemnon, son of Athens, pursued them,
> Killing without pause the hindmost; thus they fled.

In the course of the afternoon, Hector regains advantage, withdraws again, then puts the Greeks to rout, is set back in his turn by Patroclus' fresh forces. Patroclus, pushing his advantage beyond its strength, ends by finding himself exposed, unarmed, and wounded by Hector's javelin, and that evening the victorious Hector receives with severe reprimand Polydamas' prudent advice:

> 'Now that I have received from the crafty son
>   of Kronos
> A glorious victory near the ships, forcing the Greeks into
>   the sea,
> Fool! Never voice such counsel before the
>   people.
> No Trojan will listen to you; as for me, I
>   forbid it.'
> Thus spoke Hector, and the Trojans acclaimed him.

The next day Hector is lost. Achilles has pushed him back across the whole plain and will kill him. Of the two, he has always been the stronger in combat; how much more so now after several weeks of rest and spurred on by vengeance to victory against a spent enemy! Here is Hector alone before the walls of

Troy, completely alone awaiting death and trying to gather his soul to face it.

> Alas! if I should retreat behind the gate and the
>   rampart
> Polydamas would be first to shame me. . . .
> Now that by my folly I have destroyed my people,
> I fear the Trojans, and the long-robed
>   Trojan women.
> And I fear to hear it said by those less brave
>   than I:
> 'Hector, too confident of his strength, has lost
>   our land.'
> But what if I put away my arched shield,
> My stout helmet, and leaning my lance against
>   the rampart
> I went forth to meet the illustrious Achilles?
> But why now should my heart give me such counsel?
> I will not approach him; he would have no pity,
> No regard; he would kill me if I were thus naked,
> Like a woman.

Hector escapes none of the grief and ignominy that belong to the ruined. Alone, stripped of all the prestige of might, the courage that upheld him outside the walls cannot preserve him from flight:

> Hector, at the sight of him was seized with
>   trembling. He could not resolve
> To remain. . . .
> It is not for a ewe nor for an ox-hide,
> Nor for the ordinary compensations of the hunt that
>   they strive.
> It is for a life that they run, that of Hector,
>   tamer of horses.

Fatally wounded, he augments the triumph of the victor by his vain entreaties.

> I implore thee by thy life, by thy knees, by thy
>   parents.

But those who are familiar with the *Iliad* know the death of Hector was to give but short-lived joy to Achilles and the death of Achilles brief joy to the Trojans, and the annihilation of Troy but brief joy to the Achaians.

For violence so crushes whomever it touches that it appears at last external no less to him who dispenses it than to him who endures it. So the idea was born of a destiny beneath which the aggressors and their victims are equally innocent, the victors and the vanquished brothers in the same misfortune. The vanquished is a cause of misfortune for the victor as much as the victor is for the vanquished.

> An only son is born to him, for a short life; moreover
> He grows old abandoned by me, since far from home
> I linger before Troy, doing harm to you and to your sons.

A moderate use of might, by which alone man may escape being caught in the machinery of its vicious circle, would demand a more than human virtue, one no less rare than a constant dignity in weakness. Further, moderation itself is not always without peril; for the prestige which constitutes three-fourths of might is first of all made up of that superb indifference which the powerful have for the weak, an indifference so contagious that it is communicated even to those who are its object. But ordinarily it is not a political idea which counsels excess. Rather is the temptation to it nearly irresistible, despite all counsels. Reasonable words are now and then pronounced in the *Iliad*; those of Thersites are reasonable in the highest degree. So are Achilles' words when he is angry:

> Nothing is worth life to me, not all the rumoured
>   wealth of Ilium, that so prosperous city. . . .
> For one may capture oxen and fat sheep
> But a human life, once lost, is not to be recaptured.

Reasonable words fall into the void. If an inferior pronounced them he is punished and turns silent. If a leader, he does not put them into action. If need be he is always able to find a god to counsel him the opposite of reason. At last the very idea that one might wish to escape from the occupation bestowed by fate, that to kill and to be killed, disappears from the consciousness.

> . . . we, to whom Zeus
> From our youth to old age, has assigned the struggle
> In painful wars, until we perish even to the last one. . . .

Already these combatants, as so much later Craonne's, felt themselves 'wholly condemned'.

They are caught in this situation by the simplest of traps. At the outset their hearts are light, as hearts always are when one feels power within one and against one only the void. Their weapons are in their hands; the enemy is absent. Unless one's soul is stricken by the enemy's reputation, one is always stronger than he during his absence. An absent enemy does not impose the yoke of necessity. As yet no necessity appears in the consciousness of those who thus set forth, and this is why they go off as if to a game, as if for a holiday freed from the daily grind.

> Where have our braggings gone, our vaunted bravery,
> Which we shouted so proudly at Lemnos
> While gorging upon the flesh of horned bullocks,
> And drinking from cups overflowing with wine?
> Saying: against an hundred or two hundred Trojans
> Each one would hold combat; and here only one is
>   too much for us!

Even when war is experienced, it does not immediately cease to appear as a game. The necessity that belongs to war is terrible, wholly different from that belonging to peaceful works; the soul only submits to the necessity of war when escape from it is impossible; and so long as the soul does escape, it lives irresponsible days, empty of necessity, days of frivolity, of dream, arbitrary and unreal. Danger is then an abstraction, the lives which one takes seem like toys broken by a child, and no more important; heroism is a theatrical pose soiled by artificial braggings. If, added to this, an influx of vitality comes to multiply and inflate the power of action, the man believes that, thanks to divine intervention, he is irresistible, providentially preserved from defeat and from death. War is easy then, and ignobly loved.

But for the majority of soldiers this state of soul does not last. The day comes when fear, defeat or the death of beloved companions crushes the warrior's soul beneath the necessity of war. Then war ceases to be a play or a dream; the warrior understands at last that it really exists. This is a hard reality, infinitely too hard to be borne, for it comprises death. The thought of death cannot be sustained, or only in flashes from the moment when one understands death as a possible eventuality. It is true that every man is destined to die and that a soldier may grow old among his comrades, yet for those whose souls are subservient to the yoke of war, the relationship between death and the future is different than for other men. For those others death is the acknowledged limit pre-imposed upon their future; for these warriors, death itself is their future, the future assigned to them by their profession. That men should have death for their future is a denial of nature. As soon as the practice of war has revealed the fact that each moment holds the possibility of death, the mind becomes incapable of moving from one day to the next without passing through the spectre of death. Then the consciousness is under tension such as it can only endure for short intervals. But each new dawn ushers in the same necessity. Such days added to each other make up years. That soul daily suffers violence which every morning must mutilate its aspirations because the mind cannot move about in a time without passing through death. In this way war wipes out every conception of a goal, even all thoughts concerning the goals of war. The possibility of so violent a situation is inconceivable when one is outside it, its ends are inconceivable when one is involved in it. Therefore no one does anything to bring about its end. The man who is faced by an armed enemy cannot lay down his arms. The mind should be able to contrive an issue; but it has lost all capacity for contriving anything in that direction. It is completely occupied with doing itself violence. Always among men, the intolerable afflictions either of servitude or war endure by force of their own weight, and therefore, from the outside, they seem easy to bear; they last because they rob the resources required to throw them off.

Nevertheless, the soul that is dominated by war cries out for deliverance; but deliverance itself appears in tragic guise, in the form of extreme destruction. A moderate and reasonable end to all its suffering would leave naked, and exposed to consciousness, memories of such violent affliction as it could not endure. The terror, the pain, the exhaustion, the massacres, the deaths of comrades, we cannot believe that these would only cease to ravage the soul if they were drowned in the intoxication of force. The thought that such vast efforts should have brought only a negative, or limited profit, hurts too much.

> What? Shall we allow Priam and the Trojans, to glory
> In Argive Helen, she for whom so many Greeks
> Have perished before Troy, far from their native
>   land?
> What? Would you abandon Troy, the city of wide streets,
> For which we have suffered so many afflictions?

What does Helen matter to Ulysses? Or even Troy with all its wealth, since it can never compensate for the ruin of Ithaca? Troy and Helen matter to the Greeks only as the causes of their shedding so much blood and tears; it is in making oneself master that one finds one is the master of horrible memories. The Soul, which is forced by the existence of an enemy, to destroy the part of itself implanted by nature, believes it can only cure itself by the destruction of the enemy, and at the same time the death of beloved companions stimulates the desire to emulate them, to follow their dark example:

> Ah, to die at once, since without my help
> My friends had to die. How far from home
> He perished, and I was not there to defend him.
> Now I depart to find the murderer of one so beloved:

42

Hector. I will receive death at whatever moment
Zeus and all the other gods shall accomplish it.

So it is that the despair which thrusts toward death is the same
one that impels toward killing.

I know well that my fate is to perish here,
Far from my loved father and mother; but still
I will not stop till the Trojans have had their
    glut of war.

The man torn by this double need for death belongs, so long as
he has not become something different, to another race than
the living race. When the vanquished pleads that he may be
allowed to see the light of day, what echo may his timid aspiration
to life find in a heart driven by such desperation? The mere fact
that the victor is armed, the other disarmed, already deprives the
life that is threatened of the least vestige of importance. And how
should he who has destroyed in himself the very thought that
there may be joy in the light, how should he respect such humble
and vain pleadings from the vanquished?

I am at thy knees, Achilles; have pity, have regard
    for me;
Here as a suppliant, O Son of Zeus, I am worthy of
    respect:
It was first at your house that I ate the bread of
    Demeter,
When from my well-tended vineyard you captured me.
And selling me, you sent me far from my father and
    my own,
To holy Lemnos; a sacrifice of one hundred oxen were
    paid for me.
I was redeemed for three hundred more; Dawn breaks
    for me
Today the twelfth time since I returned to Ilium
After so many sorrows. Again at the mercy of your
    hands

> A cruel fate has placed me. How Zeus the father
>> must hate me
> To have delivered me to you again; for how small
>> a part in life
> Did my mother, Laothoe, daughter of the ancient
>> Altos, bear me.

See what response this feeble hope gets!

> Come friend, you must die too! Who are you to
>> complain?
> Patroclus was worth much more than you, yet he
>> is dead.
> And I, handsome and strong as you see me,
> I who am of noble race, my mother was a goddess;
> Even over me hangs death and a dark destiny.
> Whether at dawn, in the evening, or at noon
> My life too shall be taken by force of arms. . . .

Whoever has had to mortify, to mutilate in himself all aspiration to live, of him an effort of heart-breaking generosity is required before he can respect the life of another. We have no reason to suppose any of Homer's warriors capable of such an effort, unless prehaps Patroclus. In a certain way Patroclus occupies the central position in the *Iliad*, where it is said that: 'he knew how to be tender toward all', and wherein nothing of a cruel or brutal nature is ever mentioned concerning him. But how many men do we know in several thousand years of history who have given proof of such divine generosity? It is doubtful whether we could name two or three. In default of such generosity the vanquished soldier is the scourge of nature; possessed by war, he, as much as the slave, although in quite a different way, is become a thing, and words have no more power over him than over inert matter. In contact with might, both the soldier and the slave suffer the inevitable effect, which is to become either deaf or mute.

Such is the nature of might. Its power to transform man into a thing is double and it cuts both ways; it petrifies differently but equally the souls of those who suffer it, and of those who wield it. This property of might reaches its highest degree in the midst of combat, at that moment when the tide of battle feels its way toward a decision. The winning of battles is not determined between men who plan and deliberate, who make a resolution and carry it out, but between men drained of these faculties, transformed, fallen to the level either of inert matter, which is all passivity, or to the level of blind forces, which are all momentum. This is the final secret of war. This secret the *Iliad* expresses by its similes, by making warriors apparitions of great natural phenomenon: a conflagration, a flood, the wind, ferocious beasts, any and every blind cause of disaster. Or else by likening them to frightened animals, trees, water, sand, to all that is moved by the violence of external forces. Greeks and Trojans alike, from one day to the next, sometimes from one hour to the next, are made to suffer in turn these contrary transmutations.

> Like cattle which a murderous lion assaults
> While they stand grazing in a vast and marshy meadow
> By thousands . . .; all tremble. So then the Achaians
> In panic were put to rout by Hector and by Zeus the
>   father.
> All of them. . . .
> As when destructive fire runs through the depths
>   of a wood;
> Everywhere whirling, swept by the wind, when the trees
> Uprooted are felled by pressure of the violent fire;
> Even so did Agamemnon son of Athens bring down the heads
> Of the fleeing Trojans.

The art of war is nothing but the art of provoking such transformations. The material, the procedures, even the inflicting of death upon the enemy, are only the means to this end; the veritable object of the art of war is no less than the souls of the combatants. But these transformations are always a mystery, and the gods are the authors of them because it is they who excite men's imaginations. However this comes about, this double ability of turning men to stone is essential to might, and a soul placed in contact with it only escapes by a sort of miracle. Miracles of this sort are rare and brief.

The frivolity, the capriciousness of those who disrespectfully manipulate the men or the things which they have, or believe they have at their mercy, the despair which drives the soldier to destroy, the crushing of the slave and of the vanquished, the massacres, all these contribute to make a picture of utter, uniform horror. Might is the only hero in this picture. The resulting whole would be a dismal monotony were there not, sprinkled here and there, luminous moments, brief and divine moments in the souls of men. In such moments the soul which awakes, only to lose itself again to the empire of might, awakes pure and intact; realizes itself whole. In that soul there is no room for ambiguous, troubled or conflicting emotions; courage and love fill it all. Sometimes a man is able to find his soul in deliberating with himself when he tries, as Hector did before Troy, without the help of gods or of men, all alone to face his destiny. Other moments wherein men find their souls are the moments when they love; almost no type of pure love between men is lacking from the *Iliad*.

The tradition of hospitality, carried through several generations, has ascendancy over the blindness of combat:

> Thus I am for you a beloved guest in the heart of
> Argos. . . .
> Let us avoid one another's lances, even in
> the fray.

The love of a son for his parents, of a father, or of a mother, for the son, is constantly expressed in a manner as moving as it is brief:

> Thetis replied, shedding tears:
> You were born to me for a short life my child,
> as you say. . . .

Likewise fraternal love:

> My three brothers born of our same mother
> So cherished. . . .

Married love, condemned to misfortune, is of a surprising purity. The husband, in evoking the humiliations of slavery which await his beloved wife, omits to mention that one of which only to think would be to forecast memories that would soil their tenderness. Nothing could be more simple than the words spoken by his wife to the husband who goes to his death:

> . . . It were better for me
> If I lose you, to be under the ground, I shall have
> No other refuge, when you have met your fate,
> Nothing but griefs.

No less moving are the words addressed to the dead husband:

> You are dead before your time, my husband; so
>   young, and I your widow
> Am left alone in the house; with our child still
>   very little,
> Whom we bore, you and I, the ill-fated. And I
>   doubt
> He will ever grow up. . . .
> For you did not die in bed stretching
>   your hands to me,
> Nor spoke one wise word that for always
> I might think on, while shedding tears day
>   and night.

The most beautiful friendship, that between companions in combat, is the final theme of the epic.

> . . . But Achilles
> Wept, dreaming of his much-loved companion;
>   and sleep
> That overcomes all, would not take him; as he
>   turned himself from side to side.

But the triumph, the purest love of all, the supreme grace of all wars, is that friendship which mounts up to brim the hearts of mortal enemies. This quells the hunger to avenge the death of a son, of a friend. It spans, by an even greater miracle, the breach that lies between the benefactor and the suppliant, between the victor and the vanquished.

> But when the desire to drink and to eat was appeased,
> Then Dardanian Priam began to admire Achilles;
> How mighty and handsome he was; he had the look
> of a god.
> And Dardanian Priam, in turn, was admired by
> Achilles,
> Who gazed at his beautiful visage and drank in
> his words.
> And when both were assuaged by their contemplation
> of each other. . . .

Such moments of grace are rare in the *Iliad*, but they suffice to make what violence kills, and shall kill, felt with extremest regret

And yet such an accumulation of violences would be cold without that accent of incurable bitterness which continually makes itself felt, although often indicated only by a single word, sometimes only by a play of verse, by a run over line. It is this which makes the *Iliad* a unique poem, this bitterness, issuing from its tenderness, and which extends, as the light of the sun, equally over all men. Never does the tone of the poem cease to be impregnated by this bitterness, nor does it ever descend to the level of a complaint. Justice and love, for which there can hardly be a place in this picture of extremes and unjust violence, yet shed their light over the whole without ever being discerned otherwise than by the accent. Nothing precious is despised, whether or not destined to perish. The destitution and misery of all men is shown without dissimulation or disdain, no man is held either above or below the common level of all men, and whatever is destroyed is regretted. The victors and the vanquished are shown equally near to us, in an equal perspective, and seem, by that token, to be the fellows as well of the poet as of the auditors. If there is a difference it is the affliction of the enemy which is perhaps the more keenly felt.

> Thus he fell there, overcome by a sleep of bronze,
> The ill-fated, far from his wife, while defending
> his people. . . .

What a tone to use in evoking the fate of the adolescent whom Achilles sold at Lemnos!

> Eleven days his heart rejoiced among those he loved
> Returning from Lemnos; on the twelfth once again
> God delivered him into the hands of Achilles,
> who would
> Send him to Hades, although against his will.

And the fate of Euphorbus, he who saw but a single day of war:

> Blood drenches his hair, hair like that of the Graces.

When Hector is mourned:

> . . . the guardian of chaste wives and of little
> children.

These words are enough to conjure up a picture of chastity ruined by violence and of little children taken by force of arms. The fountain at the gates of Troy becomes an object of piercing nostalgia when the condemned Hector passes it running to save his life.

> There were the wide wash basins, quite near,
> Beautiful, all of stone, where splendid vestments,
> Were washed by the wives of Troy and by its most
> beautiful daughters,
> Formerly, during the peace, before the advent of
> the Achaeans.
> It was this way that they ran, fleeing, and the
> other following behind.

The whole *Iliad* is overshadowed by the greatest of griefs that can come among men; the destruction of a city. This affliction

could not appear more rending if the poet had been born in Troy.
Nor is there a difference in tone in those passages which tell of the
Achaeans dying far from home.

The brief evocations of the world of peace are painful just
because that life, the life of the living, appears so full and calm:

> As soon as it was dawn and the sun rose,
> From both sides blows were exchanged and men fell.
> But at the very hour when the woodsman goes home to
>   prepare his meal
> From the valleys and hills, when his arms are wearied
> From cutting down great trees,
>   and a great longing floods his heart,
> And a hunger for sweet food gnaws at his entrails,
> At that hour, by their valour, the Danaans broke
>   the front.

All that has no part in war, all that war destroys or threatens,
the *Iliad* envelopes in poetry; this it never does for the facts of
war. The passage from life to death is veiled by not the least
reticence.

> Then his teeth were knocked out; from both sides
> Blood came to his eyes; blood that from his lips
>   and nostrils
> He vomited, open-mouthed; death wrapped him in
>   its black cloud.

The cold brutality of the facts of war is in no way disguised
just because neither victors nor vanquished are either admired,
despised or hated. Destiny and the gods almost always decide the
changing fate of the combatants. Within the limits assigned by
fate, the gods have sovereign power to mete out victory and
defeat; it is always they who provoke the madness, the treachery,
by which, each time, peace is inhibited. War is their particular
province and their only motives are caprice and malice. As for
the warriors themselves, the similes which make them appear,
victors or vanquished, as beasts or things, they cannot make us

feel either admiration or disdain, but only sorrow that men could be thus transformed.

The extraordinary equity which inspires the *Iliad* may have had other examples unknown to us; it has had no imitators. One is hardly made to feel that the poet is a Greek and not a Trojan. The tone of the poem seems to carry direct proof of the origin of the most ancient passages; although history may never give us light thereon. If one believes with Thucydides that eighty years after the destruction of Troy the Achaeans in turn were conquered, one may wonder whether these songs, in which iron is so rarely mentioned, may not be the chants of a conquered people of whom perhaps some were exiled. Obliged to live and to die 'very far from the homeland' like the Greeks before Troy, having, like the Trojans, lost their cities, they saw their likeness in the victors, who were their fathers, and also in the vanquished, whose sufferings resembled their own. Thus the truth of this war, though still recent, could appear to them as in the perspective of years, unveiled either by the intoxication of pride or of humiliation. They could picture it to themselves at once as the fallen and as the conquerors, and thus understand what never the defeated nor the victorious have ever understood, being blinded by one or the other state. This is only a dream; one can hardly do more than dream about a time so far distant.

By whatever means, this poem is a miraculous object. The bitterness of it is spent upon the only true cause of bitterness: the subordination of the human soul to might, which is, be it finally said, to matter. That subordination is the same for all mortals, although there is a difference according to the soul's degree of virtue, according to the way in which each soul endures it. No one in the *Iliad* is spared, just as no one on earth escapes it. None of those who succumb to it is for that reason despised. Whatever, in the secret soul and in human relations, can escape the empire of might, is loved, but painfully loved because of the danger of destruction that continually hangs over it. Such is the spirit of the only veritable epic of the western world. The *Odyssey* seems to be no more than an excellent imitation, now of the *Iliad*, then of some oriental poem. The *Aeneid* is an imitation which, for all its brilliance is marred by coldness, pomposity and bad taste. The *chansons de geste* were not able to attain grandeur for want of a sense of equity. In the *Chanson de Roland* the death of an enemy is not felt by the author and the reader in the same way as the death of Roland.

Attic tragedy, at least that of Aeschylus and of Sophocles, is the true continuation of the epic. Over this the idea of justice sheds its light without ever intervening; might appears here in all its rigidity and coldness, always accompanied by its fatal results from which neither he who uses it, nor he who suffers it, can escape. Here the humiliation of a soul that is subject to constraint is neither disguised, nor veiled by a facile piety; neither is it an object of disdain. More than one being, wounded by the degradation of affliction, is here held up to be admired. The Gospels are the last and most marvellous expression of Greek genius, as the *Iliad* is its first expression. The spirit of Greece makes itself felt here not only by the fact of commanding us to seek to the exclusion of every other good 'the kingdom of God and his righteousness' but also by its revelation of human misery, and by revealing that misery in the person of a divine being who is at the same time human. The accounts of the Passion show that a divine spirit united to the flesh is altered by affliction, trembles before suffering and death, feels himself, at the moment of deepest agony, separated from men and from God. The sense of human misery gives these accounts of the Passion that accent of simplicity which is the stamp of Greek genius. And it is this same sense which constitutes the great worth of Attic tragedy and of the *Iliad*. Certain expressions in the Gospels have a strangely familiar ring, reminiscent of the epic. The adolescent Trojan, sent against his will to Hades, reminds one of Christ when he told St. Peter: 'Another shall gird thee and carry thee where thou wouldst not.' This accent is inseparable from the idea which inspired the Gospels; for the understanding of human suffering is dependent upon justice, and love is its condition. Whoever does not know just how far necessity and a fickle fortune hold the human soul under their domination cannot treat as his equals, nor love as himself, those whom chance has separated from him by an abyss. The diversity of the limitations to which men are subject creates the illusion that there are different species among them which cannot communicate with one another. Only he who knows the empire of might and knows how not to respect it is capable of love and justice.

The relations between the human soul and destiny; to what extent each soul may mould its own fate; what part in any and every soul is transformed by a pitiless necessity, by the caprice of variable fortune; what part of the soul, by means of virtue and grace, may remain whole—all these are a subject in which deception is easy and tempting. Pride, humiliation, hate, disdain, indifference, the wish to forget or to ignore—all these contribute toward that temptation. Particularly rare is a true expression of misfortune: in painting it one almost always affects to believe, first, that degradation is the innate vocation of the unfortunate; second, that a soul may suffer affliction without being marked by it, without changing all consciousness in a particular manner which belongs to itself alone. For the most part the Greeks had such strength of soul as preserved them from self-deception. For this they were recompensed by knowing in all things how to attain the highest degree of lucidity, of purity and of simplicity. But the spirit which is transmitted from the *Iliad* to the Gosepls, passed on by the philosophers and tragic poets, has hardly gone beyond the limits of Greek civilization. Of that civilization, since the destruction of Greece, only reflections are left.

The Romans and the Hebrews both believed themselves exempt from the common misery of man, the Romans by being chosen by destiny to be the rulers of the world, the Hebrews by the favour of their God, and to the exact extent in which they obeyed Him. The Romans despised foreigners, enemies, the vanquished, their subjects, their slaves; neither have they any epics or tragedies. The Hebrews saw a trace of sin in all affliction and therefore a legitimate motive for despising it. They saw their vanquished as an abomination in God's sight and therefore condemned to expiate their crimes. Thus cruelty was sanctioned and even inevitable. Nor does any text of the Old Testament sound a note comparable to that of the Greek epic, unless perhaps certain parts of the poem of Job. The Romans and Hebrews have been admired, read, imitated in actions and in words, cited every time there was need to justify a crime, throughout twenty centuries of Christianity.

Furthermore, the spirit of the Gospels was not transmitted in all its purity to successive generations of Christians. From the earliest times it was believed to be a sign of grace when the martyrs joyfully endured suffering and death; as if the effects of grace could be realized more fully among men than in the Christ. Those who remember that even the incarnate God Himself could not look on the rigours of destiny without anguish, should understand that men can only appear to elevate themselves above human misery by disguising the rigours of destiny in their own eyes, by the help of illusion, of intoxication, or of fanaticism. Unless protected by an armour of lies, man cannot endure might without suffering a blow in the depth of his soul. Grace can prevent this blow from corrupting the soul, but cannot prevent its wound. For having too long forgotten this the Christian tradition has been able only very rarely to find that simplicity which makes each phrase of the accounts of the Passion so poignant.

Despite the brief intoxication caused, during the Renaissance, by the discovery of Greek letters, the Greek genius has not been revived in the course of twenty centuries. Something of it appears in Villon, Shakespeare, Cervantes, Molière, and once in Racine. In the *École des Femmes*, in *Phèdre*, human misery is revealed in its nakedness in connection with love. That was a strange century in which, contrary to what happened in the epic age, man's misery could only be revealed in love. The effects of might in war and in politics had always to be enveloped in glory. Doubtless one could add still other names. But nothing of all that the peoples of Europe have produced is worth the first known poem to have appeared among them. Perhaps they will rediscover that epic genius when they learn how to accept the fact that nothing is sheltered from fate, how never to admire might, or hate the enemy, or to despise sufferers. It is doubtful if this will happen soon.

V

ZEUS AND PROMETHEUS[1]

Aeschylus, *Agamemnon*, 160–183

Ζεύς, ὅστις ποτ' ἐστίν, εἰ τόδ' αὐτῷ φίλον κεκλημένῳ
τοῦτό νιν προσεννέπω. . . .

Zeus, whoever he may be, if by this name it pleases him
to be invoked,
By this name I call him.
Nothing is left that I can compare with him, having weighed all
things,
Except Zeus,
If I am to cast this vain burden of anxiety from me.
Nor shall he who was great long ago, bursting with a victor's
boldness,
Be said even to have existed,
Nor shall he who followed, and has disappeared in finding
his vanquisher.
But whoever, with thoughts turned to Zeus, shall cry his glory,
Shall receive the fullness of wisdom.

He has opened the way of wisdom to mortals, proclaiming as
sovereign law:
By suffering comes understanding.

[1] From *La Source Grecque*, pages 43-47.

56

So accrues to the heart, drop by drop, during sleep,
The wage of dolorous memory;
And even without willing it, wisdom comes.
From the gods who sit at the celestial helm,
    grace comes violently.

This passage from a chorus of the *Agamemnon* of Aeschylus, which as Greek is difficult and almost untranslatable, is interesting as being one of those which obviously reflects the doctrine taught to the initiates of the Mysteries, notably that of Eleusis. The tragedies of Aeschylus are clearly impregnated by this doctrine. Zeus seems to be regarded therein as the supreme God, that is to say, the only God, and as being above all the God of Moderation, and of the chastisements that punish excess, the excess and the abuse of power under all their forms. To understand is presented as the supreme end, that is, of course, to understand the relationship of man and the universe, of men among themselves, of man with himself. According to this passage, suffering was regarded as the indispensable condition for such knowledge, and precious by this token, but by this token only. Unlike certain morbid valuations of our time, the Greeks never attributed value to suffering for its own sake. The word they chose to designate suffering, πάθος, is one which evoked above all the idea of *enduring* much more than of suffering. Man must endure that which he does not want. He must find himself in submission to necessity. Misfortunes leave wounds which bleed drop by drop even during sleep; and thus, little by little, they break a man by violence and make him fit, in spite of himself, to receive wisdom, that wisdom which expresses itself as moderation. Man must learn to think of himself as a limited and dependent being, suffering alone can teach him this.

Tῷ πάθει μάθος is evidently an equation sanctioned by the adepts of the doctrine which Aeschylus echoed and which is doubtless Orphism. The resemblance of the two words πάθος, μάθος makes of this equation a sort of play on words. Equations of this sort were prized by the Greek initiates; compare the σῶμα σῆμα of the

Pythagoreans (the body is a tomb). Further on, the same choir chants Δίκα δὲ τοῖς μὲν παθοῦσιν μαθεῖν ἐπιρρέπει, justice makes fall to the share (Δίκα = justice, ἐπιρρέπω = to make fall [in the sense of 'to weigh out' trans.]—or, rather, justice grants understanding to those who have suffered, or, grants knowledge.

I would almost prefer to put 'those who have endured', instead of those who have suffered, to underline that those who know are those who have endured misfortune, not those who have taken pleasure in tormenting themselves by pure perversity or by romanticism. 'Ἐπιρρέπει indicates that those who have suffered may share in the possibility of knowing only if they use this possibility. This equation does not of course mean to say that suffering automatically yields wisdom.

By its very colour this passage clearly reveals the origin of its inspiration to be that of the Mysteries. (The two solitary divinities are certainly not, as affirmed in a note by an unfortunate Sorbonne professor, those of Hesiodic or Orphic genealogy, but false gods anterior to a revelation, which for the Greeks is probably that brought in by contact with the Pelasgians, the Phoenicians and the Egyptians.) These lines contain the sufficient and infallible method of perfection, which is to keep the mind turned in loving contemplation towards the true God, that God who has no name. The 'dolorous memory' is Plato's reminiscence, the remembrance of what the soul saw upon the farther side of heaven; that dolorous memory which distils in sleep, is the 'dark night' of St. John of the Cross.

If one compares lines from the *Prometheus*, the similarity of the story of Prometheus with that of the Christ appears with blinding evidence. Prometheus is the preceptor of men, who has taught them all things. Here he (the preceptor) is said to be Zeus. That is all the same thing; the two are really one. It is in crucifying Prometheus that Zeus has opened the way of wisdom to men.

Henceforth the law, 'by suffering comes understanding', may be brought in line with the thought of St. John of the Cross: that participation in the suffering of the Cross of Christ alone allows penetration into the depths of divine wisdom.

Moreover, if one compares the first lines spoken by Prometheus[1] with the end of the Book of Job,[2] one sees in these two texts the same mysterious linking between extreme physical suffering, accompanied by an extreme distress of soul, and the complete revelation of the beauty of the world.

*   *   *

Compare certain lines from the sixth-century Pythagorean comic poet Epicharmus on the subject of the folly of love with a verse from the *Prometheus* of Aeschylus spoken by Ocean:

'The matter with you is not the love of mankind, but an illness; that you find joy in giving.'[3]

The line spoken by Ocean is as follows:

'There is no greater gain than to appear mad because one is good.'

Prometheus replies:

'That fault would seem rather to be mine.'   (*Prometheus*, 385-6.)

---

[1] 'O divine heaven, swift wings of wind,
O rivers and their springs, O seas
and numberless smiling waves, and thou, Mother of all, Earth,
and that one who sees all, disk of the sun, I call upon you
to see in me what sufferings the gods bring to a god.'

(*Prometheus*, 88-92)

[2] Job, xxxviii-xli.

[3] οὐ φιλάνθρωπος γ' ἔσσ', ἔχεις νόσον, χαίρεις διδούς.
      Diels, *Fragmente der Vorsokratiker*, 5th ed., I, 203, fr. 31.

VI

PROMETHEUS[1]

THE EXACT MEANING of the name Prometheus is Providence. Hesiod relates that Prometheus was the arbiter at a contest between the gods and men (ἐκρίνοντο θεοὶ θνητόι τ' ἄνθρωποι: *Theogony*, 535) to decide which share of the sacrificial animals should fall to the gods and which to men; he relates that Prometheus gave the better part to men.

This recalls an extraordinary passage in the Book of Job (xvi, 19-21): 'Also now, behold, my witness is in heaven, and my record is on high. My friends scorn me: but mine eye poureth out tears unto God. O that one might plead for a man with God, as a man pleadeth for his neighbour!' (King James Version). 'O that God himself might be the arbiter between man and God, between the son of man and his fellows' (French Version).

Aeschylus first shows the crucifixion of Prometheus upon the rock, during which Prometheus is completely silent. This recalls the silence of Isaiah's just man and the silence of the Christ: 'He was oppressed, and he was afflicted, yet he opened not his mouth' (Isaiah liii, 7).

From the moment that Prometheus is alone, he has an explosion of pain which leaves no doubt as to the carnal character of his suffering.

Aeschylus also makes it clear that he suffers for love. From the *Prometheus Bound*:

[1] From, *Les Intuitions Préchrétiennes*, pages 93-108.

60

Divine heaven, swift wings of wind,   89
O rivers and their springs, O seas and numberless
smiling waves, and thou, mother of all, Earth,
and he who sees all, orb of the sun, I call upon you
to see in me what suffering the gods bring to a god.
Behold by what humiliations
I am torn, and must struggle throughout thousands of years.
It is this the new master of the blest
has devised for me; degrading fetters.
Alas, alas, the present and the future of my affliction
wring groans from me. At what point in my pains
shall an end be assigned to all of this?
And yet, what do I say? All this I knew in advance,   101
exactly, all the future. Nothing new for me can come
to add to my affliction. Since it is destined, one's lot
must be endured the best one can; I know well
that invincible necessity is in power.
But neither keeping silent nor failing to keep silent
is possible in this state. To mortals I have given
a grace, and these laws master me, their victim.
In the hollow of a rod I captured
the stolen source of fire, who teaches skill,
shows all skill to mortals and is a great treasure.
It is the ransom of this fault that I pay,
in the open air, enchained and nailed. . . .
Behold me enchained, a miserable god   119
whom Zeus hates, whom all the gods
hold in horror, all those who
attend the court of Zeus,
because I have loved mortals too well.
Alas, alas, what movements do I hear
of birds close by? Upon the air the whirr
of beating wings rustles gently.
All that comes near is frightening to me. . . .
                      . . . see   141
how I am held by a hook!
Above this abyss, upon this rocky height,
my lot shall be the watch that none can envy. . . .

If only beneath the earth, under the dwelling of Hades, 152
welcomer of corpses, in that immensity
of Tartarus, he had flung me! Though unbreakable chains
should cruelly hold me, yet no god,
nor any other being, could take pleasure.
But here, wretchedly battered by the wind,
my enemies exult over my suffering. . . .
His [Zeus] will shall soften one day, when 187
as I have said, he shall be shattered; he, the inflexible,
he shall appease his anger; in union with me
and in friendship
he shall hasten to me as I hasten to him. . . .
They [the Titans] believed that without trouble, by force,
they should be masters. . . . 208
They deigned not the least in the world to look upon
me. . . . 215
[The best] seemed to take my mother with me
and to consent to be allied with Zeus, who consented to it.
It was by my advice . . . 219
  [that they had the victory]
. . . the unhappy mortals; he took no account of them, 231
none at all; on the contrary, his wish was to destroy
  the species
completely, and to sow a new race.
And to that none made opposition, but only I
have dared. I have delivered mortals
from the damnation that would have flung them into Hades.
It is for this fault these tortures crush me.
They are bitter to suffer and pitiable to see.
For mortals I have had pity, while to myself, none
deigns to accord pity, but fierce, fierce
is the measure that I receive here, an inglorious
  spectacle before Zeus. . . .
and certainly to my friends I am a lamentable sight. . . . 246
I caused mortals no longer to foresee the day of doom. 248
CHORUS: What remedy did you invent for this illness?
PROMETHEUS: I caused blind hopes to dwell in them. . .
  [after a new evocation of his sufferings]

62

and I, all these things, I knew them, 265
I consented, I consented to be in the wrong, I'll not
    deny it.
To mortals I brought succour and found sufferings
    for myself.
However, I had not thought to pay such a ransom,
not wasted away, upon these high cliffs
to have the desert and this abandoned mountain for
    my lot. . . .
See this spectacle, this friend of Zeus 304
who helped to establish his kingdom,
beneath what tortures he makes me bow! . . .

OCEAN: Nothing is better than to will good for others 385
    to the point of appearing mad.
PROMETHEUS: It is I who appear to be in that error. . . .
OCEAN: Thy calamity, O Prometheus, is a lesson. . . . 391
PROMETHEUS: One thought gnaws at my heart, 437
    that I see how I have been outraged
and yet, who determined the privileges
of these new gods, if not I alone? . . .
        . . . Of the afflictions of mortals 442
hear these, and how, knowing nothing at first,
I endowed them with a mind and the possession of
    wisdom.
I will say it, not in any way to blame men,
but to show what there was of goodness in my gifts.
They, who at first, when they saw, saw in vain,
heard without understanding; and resembling
the figures in dreams, the whole of length their life
they confused all things at random. . . .
All these inventions, I, unhappy one, found them 469
for mortals; and for myself I have no wisdom which can,
from this present torture, deliver me now.
CHORUS: You suffer a painful humiliation. Fallen
    from your wisdom
you err, like a bad physician succumbed to
sickness. You have lost courage and
    for yourself are not able

to decide by which potions to cure yourself. . . .

PROMETHEUS: In a single word learn the whole at once: 503
all mortal arts come from Prometheus.

CHORUS: Be not useful to mortals above measure,
and careless of your own misfortune; as for me
I have good hope that one day delivered from these bonds
you shall be not inferior to Zeus
in power. . . .

CHORUS: You do not tremble before Zeus, and   543
following your own will, you venerate mortals too
much, Prometheus.

PROMETHEUS: Behold Prometheus, giver of fire to   612
mortals.

IO: O thou, who hast shown thyself the universal benefactor of
mortals
unhappy Prometheus, for what reason do you suffer thus?

PROMETHEUS: I have just concluded the account of my pains.

IO: Then give me this one grace.

PROMETHEUS: Say which one. You may ask me any question. . . .

PROMETHEUS: In reality there is before me no end to my   755
torments until Zeus fall from royal power.

IO: Zeus fall from power, is that possible? . . .

PROMETHEUS: You may accept that as reality.   760

IO: By whom shall he be robbed of his royal sceptre?

PROMETHEUS: Himself by himself and by his designs
empty of wisdom. . . .
He shall make such a marriage as he shall be ashamed of. . . .   764
His wife shall bring the world a son stronger than   768
his father.

IO: Is there nothing that can turn this fate from him?

PROMETHEUS: No, nothing, except myself, if I were freed from
my chains. . . .

PROMETHEUS: Yes, it is a fact, no longer a saying: 1080
The earth is shaken
subterranean echoes roar in reply
to the thunder, and to the flaring lines
of fiery lightning; in the eddies the dust

whirls; winds leap up breaking
winds, all are against each other;
a war of winds is declared.
There is a confounding of sky and ocean.
Against me the tempest from Zeus,
bringing terror advances visible.
O my mother and her holiness, O heaven,
by whom the common light of all turns,
do you see what wrongs I suffer?

These words are the last of the tragedy. It finishes with the word πάσχω so near to the Passion.

He had pity and received no pity. Antigone also says, in Sophocles' play, that having shown piety she suffered impious treatment. The Greeks were haunted by the thought that caused a saint of the Middle Ages to weep: the thought that Love is not loved.

The vocabulary of this tragedy presents many oddities, rare words, which are doubtless words of double meaning to which we have lost the key. The key ought to be in the liturgy of the Mysteries. Concerning the words πόρος and μηχανή which reappear constantly and must, here and in the other works in which they figure, be an allusion to that liturgy.

Some probable allusions to Aeschylus' tragedy, or to a common source in Plato's *Symposium*, have been noted earlier. Prometheus is without a roof, exposed to the rigours of the open air, so is Love. Prometheus, at the hunt, captured the source of fire. Love is also a mighty huntsman. Prometheus is a physician who cannot find a cure for himself. Love is a physician who cures the evil that robs man of the supreme felicity. Love is skilful in finding potions. There are still other comparisons to be made. But above all, Love does not exercise nor submit to constraint. The relations between Prometheus and Zeus are of this sort, contrary to what the nails and the chains might lead one to believe. Their relations are of the type indicated by such grammatical constructions as ἑκόνθ' ἑκόντι, σπεύδων σπεύδοντι. Plato also says ἑκὼν ἑκόντι. The

Pythagorean character of the thought which inspires Aeschylus' drama is indicated by several signs. When Prometheus explains how his educative action brought men out of their state of confused nightmare, he enumerates the kinds of knowledge that he gave them. These are, in the poet's order, the construction of houses; work with bricks and wood; the knowledge of the seasons; that of the stars; and of numbers; and of letters; the domestication of the horse; navigation by sailboat; medicine; divination; sacrifices; work with metals—briefly, all the arts. In this slightly confused enumeration, the knowledge of numbers is called ἔξοχον σοφισμάτων, the wisdom which surpasses all others. This is a specifically Pythagorean idea.

Be it said in passing (although the Bible I believe says somewhere that it is from Wisdom that men learned ploughing and all the crafts) such thoughts are completely lacking among us today. And yet, if we thought of all the techniques as gifts from Christ, would not all of life be transformed by that belief?

When Prometheus speaks of his future reconciliation with Zeus, he uses the word ἀρθμόν, union (190), a very rare word and which must be used here as a sort of play on words with ἀριθμόν, number. When he says ὡς ἐρρύθμισμαι, it is certainly because Aeschylus wants to invoke the idea of rhythm that to say 'this is the way one treats me' he so fantastically seeks out a word derived from ῥυθμός. Elsewhere Prometheus begins a phrase by ἁρμοῖ, which means 'in a little while'. This is also a rare word, the adverbial dative of the word which means 'adjusting, dovetailing', coming from the same root as harmony.

What is more important is that Prometheus speaks of having determined the privileges of the gods, of having prescribed their limits, διώρισεν (440). This bears directly upon the Pythagorean ideas concerning the limit and the unlimited, which are the foundation of that doctrine. Upon this subject, see further on. The connection is in no way arbitrary, for Plato attributes this part of the doctrine precisely to a revelation from Prometheus. This revelation is elsewhere linked to that of the techniques.

πέτραις πεδαρσίοις, upon high cliffs [from αἴρω].

This expression recalls 'the Son of man must be lifted up'.

αἰθέριον κίνυγμα, a thing buffeted about by the winds.

That doubtless means exposed to the elements. However, the expression is strange for a body nailed to a rock. It would be more appropriate for a hanging body. Here one might believe that to the torture of crucifixion Aeschylus superimposes the torture of hanging. For mysterious reasons the Christian tradition has always done the same for the Christ (hanged on a tree, hanged upon the Cross).

Prometheus suffers because he has loved men too well. He suffers in man's stead, The wrath of God against the human species is entirely carried by him, who, nevertheless, was and is, destined again to become the friend of Zeus.

He who, by his counsels, secured the reign of Zeus, who distributed to the gods their portions and their functions, all of which belongs to the sovereign ruler, he whom one expects to see as equal to Zeus in power, reduces himself to total powerlessness. Left in a deserted place where none can speak to him or hear him (if in the actual tragedy he has interlocutors, that is because such are necessary for the theatre), secured by nails and chains in complete immobility, in an unnatural position, unable to satisfy the need to hide himself which is so terribly intense in humiliation and affliction, exposed to the sight of whoever may happen to come to mock his distress, he is hated by the gods, abandoned by men.

He had no fear of Zeus, and he venerated men. The very power of his will for good proved him mad. (All these expressions are in the text.)

His gifts to humanity are first of all salvation, in that he prevented their annihilation by Zeus. He does not say how, but it is for this that he suffers. Then he gave them fire and knowledge of the order of the world, and of numbers and of techniques. But he has also freed men from the fear of death by filling them with

blind hopes. Blind is used here as the night of faith in St. John of
the Cross. It is the hope of immortality. This brings Prometheus
in line with the Egyptian Osiris, the god of immortality.

But he who delivered men cannot deliver himself.

And yet, all powerless as he is, he is in a sense more powerful
than Zeus. There is something very singular about Zeus in this
tragedy. Everywhere else in Aeschylus the essential attribute of
Zeus is Wisdom. He is only secondarily powerful, just, good, and
merciful. He is above all the Wise God. In this tragedy he lacks
wisdom to the point where this deficiency threatens the future of
his reign, he is condemned to lose his kingdom because his
'counsels are empty of wisdom', and there is no other help for
him than to deliver Prometheus from his chains.

The conclusion imposes itself upon us that Prometheus himself
is the Wisdom of Zeus. Henceforth, when we see in *Agamemnon*
that it suffices to turn one's thoughts to Zeus to obtain the
plenitude of wisdom, that Zeus has opened the way of wisdom to
mortals, and when one brings this saying in line with Prometheus'
words where he says how he has been the preceptor of men, one
is convinced that Zeus and Prometheus are one and the self-same
God; and one must interpret the words 'He decreed as sovereign
law: By suffering comes understanding' as a link with the passion
of Prometheus. The Christian likewise knows that he must go
by the Way of the Cross to be united with divine Wisdom.

Without Prometheus, Zeus would have a son more powerful
than himself and would thus lose his domination. It is not by
might, it is by wisdom that God is the ruler of the world.

The idea of a situation where God would be separated from his
Wisdom is very strange, But it appears also, although less insistently, in the story of Christ. The Christ accuses His Father of
having abandoned Him; and Saint Paul says that Christ has
become a curse before God in our stead. At the supreme moment
of the Passion, there is an instant where there appears a thing
which to human eyes seems a separation, an opposition between
the Father and the Son. Certainly this is no more than an appear-

ance. But in Aeschylus' tragedy, a few words scattered here and there—which doubtless would have much more significance for us if we knew the *Prometheus Unbound*—indicate that the hostility between Prometheus and Zeus is only an appearance.

See an attempted interpretation of this appearance further on, in connection with the Pythagorean idea of harmony, pages 195-199).

Prometheus has for mother a goddess who has, among other names, Themis, justice; another name is Gaia, Earth. This is the mother goddess, whom one also meets under the name of Isis, and of Demeter, she of whom Plato in the *Timaeus* speaks in mysterious terms, naming her matter, mother, nurse, door, hall-mark, describing her as always intact, though all things are born of her. It is she who was adored in several places where today a black Virgin is preserved.

As for the father of Prometheus, Aeschylus does not speak of him at all.

When Ocean says to Prometheus 'Thine affliction is a lesson', that seems at first the flat statement of a prudent thought. But a second sense appears in this speech when one brings it next the words: 'By suffering comes understanding.' There is in reality no greater teaching than that of the Cross.

All is freedom in this drama built of chains and of nails. At the beginning of the struggle between the Titans and Zeus, each of the two adversaries is free to take the wisdom of Prometheus to his side. But the Titans do not want it. They refuse it. They chose simply to use might. They do not accord Prometheus so much as a glance. This is the choice which condemns them to defeat, for destiny was to award the victory to whichever of the two adversaries should not use force alone, but also wisdom, and Gaia, Prometheus' mother, knew this. Prometheus, when the Titans turned from him, turns freely toward Zeus, who receives him freely and by his consenting becomes sovereign of the universe.

Later, it is also freely, freely and consciously, that Prometheus gives himself to affliction out of love for miserable humanity. 'I knew all that, I consented, I have consented to take the blame', ἑκών, ἑκών, ἥμαρτον.

Only at the moment when affliction falls is there no more liberty, but only constraint. Affliction then is not merely suffered by constraint but also inflicted by constraint. Instead of ἑκόνθ' ἑκόντι, one has here the equation ἄκοντα σ' ἄκων (invitum invitus) from the mouth of Hephaistos, keeper of the flame, son of Zeus, and by him charged with Prometheus' punishment. 'It is without your consent or my own that I am going to nail you.' At this moment God appears as submitting to necessity; not only God as victim but God as executioner; not only the God who has taken the form of a slave but also the God who has kept the form of the master.

But the reconciliation between Prometheus and Zeus shall again come freely from both sides: σπεύδων σπεύδοντι.

Notice that Hephaistos speaks of Prometheus as of a god of the same origin, συγγενῆ θεόν, and as his friend. He is the god of artistic fire.

The supernatural fire, the divine fire, which Prometheus gave to men, is the same which even in spite of himself leads him to his agony.

Prometheus' sacrifice never appears as a historical dated fact which might have happened at a certain point of time and at a certain place. Hesiod, although he does once speak of the deliverance of Prometheus, at another place speaks of him as being forever nailed to the rock.

The story of Prometheus is like the refraction into eternity of the Passion of Christ. Prometheus is the Lamb slain from the foundation of the world.

An historical anecdote whose central character is God cannot be refracted into eternity. Pascal speaks of 'Jesus in agony unto the end of the world.' St. John, with the sovereign authority of revealed texts, says that He has been slain since the foundation of the world. Among the resemblances between the story of

Prometheus and that of the Christ there is none that could be of an anecdotal order. They can in no case serve as arguments against the historical character of the Gospels. Consequently they can only confirm, and not weaken, the Christian dogma. Henceforth, why should anyone refuse to recognize them, since they are self-evident?

Outside the New Testament itself, and outside the liturgy of Holy Week, nowhere could there be found words so poignant as those of certain passages of this tragedy, words to express the love God bears us and the suffering linked to this love.

Is it not an extremely powerful thing to be able to say this to all the unbelievers: without the haunting of the Passion, this Greek civilization, from which you draw all your thoughts without exception, would never have existed?

There are all sorts of arguments against such a conception of history, but as soon as one enters into this one, it appears to be of such a crying truth that one can never abandon it.

Another essentially Christian conception which existed in Greek tradition, and which appears in Aeschylus, especially in the tragedy of the *Suppliants*, is the thought that the supplication of a sufferer comes from God himself, and that one cannot push the sufferer away without offending God. The Greeks stated that thought by an admirable expression, 'Zeus suppliant', not Zeus the protector of suppliants but 'Zeus the suppliant'.

Here are a few lines from the tragedy of the *Suppliants* which contains that statement:

> Ζεὺς μὲν ἀφίκτωρ ἐπίδοι προφρόνως. . . .   1

May suppliant Zeus look with mercy.

> ἱκτηρίας, ἀγάλματ᾽ αἰδοίου Διός.   192

The wands of supplication, images sacred to Zeus who has a right to our respect.

αἰδοῖος is impossible to translate. This word refers to the particular sort of respect which we owe to an unfortunate being

71

when he implores us. In the *Iliad* also this idea of respect is always joined to that of pity to express the respect to which the suppliant has a right. Thus the youthful son of Priam who falls without arms or armour into the hands of Achilles: 'I am at thy knees Achilles, have respect for me, have pity.' It is no credit to us that neither in French nor, to my knowledge, in any other modern language, have we a word to express this shade of meaning. (Notice that besides Zeus, the Suppliants also invoke:

Ἁγνόν τ' Ἀπόλλω, φυγάδ' ἀπ' οὐρανοῦ θεόν.   214

The pure Apollo, exiled god of heaven.

Apollo had been exiled from heaven after a quarrel with Zeus provoked by the resurrection of a dead person; and for this he had to descend to earth to become the servant of a man.)

βαρύς γε μέντοι Ζηνὸς Ἱκεσίου κότος.   347

Stern is the anger of Suppliant Zeus.

Does this not belong to the very same spirit as the words: 'I was an hungred and ye gave me no meat'?

Ἱκεσία Θέμις Διὸς κλαρίου.   360

The suppliant Justice, daughter of Zeus, Dispenser of fate. [Splendid expression.]

μένει τοι Ζηνὸς Ἱκταίου κότος   385
δυσπαραθέλκτους παθόντος οἴκτοις.

The anger of Suppliant Zeus awaits those
  whom the cry of a suffering being touches
    but little
  or, who are but little moved by the cry of a
  sufferer.

Ζεὺς ἑτερορρεπής.   403

Zeus who inclines to both sides.

Ὅμως δ' ἀνάγκη Ζηνὸς αἰδεῖσθαι κότον   478
ἰκτῆρος· ὕψιστος γὰρ ἐν βροτοῖς φόβος.

And yet one cannot choose but to have respect for the anger
  of Zeus
the Suppliant; for that is the cause of supreme fear
  among mortals.

There is, then, no greater sacrilege than insensitiveness toward those who suffer.

This anger of Suppliant Zeus recalls the prodigious words of the Apocalypse: 'They shall say to the mountains and to the rocks: Fall on us, and hide us from the face of him that sitteth on the throne, and from the wrath of the Lamb' (Revelation vi, 16).

VII

GOD IN PLATO[1]

Spirituality in Plato, i.e. Greek spirituality.

ARISTOTLE IS PERHAPS the only philosopher, in
the modern sense, in Greece, and he is quite outside the
Greek tradition. Plato is all that we have of Greek spirituality, and of him only the vulgarized works.

One can but surmise from the fact that a particular idea is not
found there, or not explicitly. . . . What then is Plato? A mystic,
heir to a tradition of mysticism wherein all of Greece was bathed.

The vocation of each of the peoples of antiquity: a view of
divine things (all but the Romans). Israel: God in one person.
India: assimilation of the soul with God in mystical union. China:
God's own method of operation, fullness of action which seems
inaction, fullness of presence which seems absence, emptiness and
silence. Egypt: immortality, salvation of the virtuous soul after
death by assimilation with a suffering God, dead and resurrected,
Charity toward one's neighbour. Greece (which greatly felt the
influence of Egypt): the wretchedness of man, the distance and
transcendence of God.

Greek history began with an atrocious crime: the destruction
of Troy. Far from deriving glory for itself from this crime as
nations ordinarily do, the Greeks were haunted by the memory

---

[1] From *La Source Grecque*, pages 65-77.

of it; that is, by remorse. From this they derived a sense of human misery. No other people has expressed as they have the bitterness of human misery: '

> Two cauldrons stand at the threshold of Zeus
> wherein are the gifts he bestows, the evil in one, the good
>   in the other.
> Those for whom Zeus, who delights in thunder, mixes his gifts,
> are sometimes in misfortune, sometimes in prosperity.
> The man to whom he makes evil gifts he exposes to outrage;
> A fearful need pursues him across divine earth,
> he wanders, receiving respect neither from men nor from the
>   Gods.[1]

There is no picture of human destitution more pure, more bitter and more poignant than the *Iliad*. The contemplation of human misery in its truth implies a very high spirituality.

All Greek civilization is a search for bridges to relate human misery and divine perfection. Their art, which is incomparable, their poetry, their philosophy, the sciences which they invented (geometry, astronomy, mechanics, physics, biology) are nothing but bridges. They invented (?), the idea of mediation. We have kept those bridges to look at them. Believers no less than non-believers. But we have almost no trace of Greek spirituality before Plato. And yet here are some fragments. Orphic fragment:

> Thou shalt find near the dwellings of the dead, on the left, a spring
> near which there soars an all white cypress tree.
> Do not go to that spring, do not approach it.
> Thou shalt find another which flows from the lake of memory,
> a jet of cold water. There are sentinels before it.
> Say to them: I am the daughter of Earth and of the starry sky
> but I have my beginning in heaven. This you know yourselves.
> A deadly thirst consumes me. Ah, give me quickly
> of the cold water that brims from the lake of memory.
> And they shall allow thee to drink from the divine spring
> and henceforth thou shalt reign among the heroes.[2]

---

[1] *Iliad*, XXIV, 527-533.   [2] Diels, 5th ed. I, p. 15.

75

This Memory is that very one which is the principle of Platonic reminiscence and of the 'grieving memory'[1] of Aeschylus. It is the knowledge of divine things. The white cypress tree has perhaps a connection with the Tree of the Knowledge of Good and Evil, which, according to the 'Quest of the Holy Grail', was entirely white.

This text already contains a part of Greek spirituality as one finds it in Plato. It comprises many things. That we are children of Heaven, which is to say, of God. That earthly life is a forgetting. That here below we live in forgetfulness of the supernatural and transcendant truth. Then, that the condition of salvation is thirst. We must thirst for that forgotten truth to the point of feeling that this thirst consumes us. Finally, that this thirst is certain to be quenched. If our thirst for that water is great enough, and if we know that as children of God it belongs to us to drink of it, then the water will be accorded us.

Pythagoreans: Of this heart of Greek civilization we know almost nothing, except from Plato.

Fragments from Heraclitus: Λόγος, Zeus, Eternal fire, fragment from Cleanthes.

Hippolytus of Euripides: absolute chastity as a means to mystical communion and friendship with divinity.

Plato: Two known facts concerning him.

1. That he is not a man who discovered a philosophic doctrine. Contrary to all other philosophers (without exception I believe), he constantly reiterates that he has invented nothing, that he only follows a tradition which sometimes he does, sometimes he does not, name. One must take his word for this.

He is inspired sometimes by earlier philosophers whose fragments we possess, whose systems he has assimilated into a superior synthesis, sometimes by his master Socrates, or again by some secret Greek traditions of which, except for him, we know almost nothing, the Orphic tradition, the tradition of the Mysteries of Eleusis, the Pythagorean tradition (which is the mother of Greek

---

[1] Aeschylus, *Agamemnon*, 180.

civilization) and very probably by the traditions of Egypt and other Oriental countries. We do not know whether Plato was the best of Greek spirituality; he is simply all that we have. Pythagoras and his disciples were doubtless still more marvellous.

2. Of Plato we possess only those popularized works which were destined for the larger public. They are not to be compared with the parables of the New Testament. Yet the fact that a certain idea is not found in them, or not explicitly, does not permit the conclusion that Plato and the other Greeks did not possess that idea.

We must try to penetrate to the heart of these works by basing our thought upon indications that are often brief and by assembling scattered texts.

My interpretation: that Plato is an authentic mystic and even the father of Occidental mysticism.

Texts concerning God:

His remark upon θεοί, θεός, ὁ θεός. Θεοί: Either he is joking. Or: the divinity (cf. Elohim). Or often something analogous to angels: finite beings but perfectly pure.

Theaetetus, 176a

THEODORUS: Socrates, if you could persuade everyone as you do me, there would be more peace and less evil among men.

SOCRATES: But it is not possible that evil should disappear, Theodorus. For something is always needed which is more or less the contrary of good (ὑπεναντίον). And this something cannot have its seat among the Gods, but it must circulate in the realm of mortal nature in this present world. That is why one should strive to *flee* this world as swiftly as one can. This flight is, as far as possible, an *assimilation* in God. This assimilation consists in becoming just and holy by the help of reason. But, dear friend, it is not easy to convince mankind to flee sin and seek virtue, not merely in order to appear to be good, which is the motive of the common man and which I take for an old woman's folly. The true motive is this: that God is never in any way unrighteous. He is righteous to the supreme degree and nothing resembles him more than that man among us who is the most righteous. . . . The understanding of this is true wisdom and virtue. To be ignorant of this is to be manifestly stupid and vile. All the other apparent abilities, other skills in politics, business or crafts, are coarse and mercenary. And as for those who commit injustices, whose words or whose actions are profane, it is better not to admit that they might be dangerous [clever] by [in] their wickedness. For they take pride in reproaches and believe themselves to be regarded *not* as empty beings, useless weights of the earth, but as virile and manly such as one must be to keep safe and sane in the city. To tell the truth, they are all the more what they believe themselves not to be, by not recognizing what they are. For they lack a knowledge of the punishment of injustice, and that is in all the world the thing one should the least lack. This punishment is not what they expect, not the death and the blows which sometimes wicked men do escape, but another punishment which it is impossible to escape. . . . There are in fact two patterns, one divine and blessed, the other devoid of God and wretched. But they do not perceive that this is so. Their stupidity, their utter ignorance blinds them to the fact that by their unjust behaviour they resemble the second and differ from the first. They are punished by the fact that they live a life which matches the pattern which they resemble.

Principal ideas to be drawn from this: *Flight.* Pythagoras: that he who leaves does not return (the violence of fear, June 1940)— and *Assimilation* (cf. geometry, *Epinomis*).

'God is perfectly just.' The Greeks were obsessed by the idea of justice (because of Troy?). They perished for having abandoned it. They knew two sets of ethics, one external, which is human, the other, the real one, which is supernatural, being from God, and interchangeable with the knowledge ($\gamma\nu\hat{\omega}\sigma\iota\varsigma$, a word from the Gospels) of the most exalted truth (note about the four virtues). The reward of good consists in the fact that one *is* good, the punishment of evil in the fact that one is evil, and these are a recompense and a punishment that are equally automatic (I do not judge, they condemn themselves).

(The very important consequence of this assimilation: the 'Ideas' of Plato are the thoughts of God, or God's attributes.)

Otherwise expressed: whereas in the domain of nature (including psychology) good and evil mutually and endlessly produce one another, in the spiritual domain evil only creates evil and good produces nothing but good. (The Gospels.) And that good and that evil consist solely in the contact with (contact by similarity), or the separation from, God. It is a question here of something very different from such an abstract conception of God as the human intelligence may achieve without grace; here the question is of an experimental conception.

What is this justice? How can the imitation of God by a man be possible? We have an answer. That answer is the Christ. What was Plato's answer?

The Republic, II, 360e

(Compare with *Hippolytus* of Euripides.) Let us take nothing either from the injustice of the unjust man or from the justice of the just man, but consider each one in his perfection. [Everything succeeds for the unjust.] . . . Take the just man, simple and generous, who, as Aeschylus says, does not want the appearance but the reality of justice. Let us then take away all appearance. . . . Let him be naked of all except justice that he may be proven in his justice by the fact that he be not softened (τέγγεσθαι) by dishonour and its effects, but unwavering unto death, going through life in the appearance of injustice but in the reality of justice . . . the just man being so disposed will be whipped, tortured, enchained, his eyes will be burnt out and at the end of all his sufferings he will be impaled [crucified] then he will know that what he should desire is not the reality, but the appearance of justice.

Adeimantus would have us also subtract questions of salvation and damnation:

The Republic, II, 367b

Do not only demonstrate to us that justice is worth more than injustice, but by what process each by itself makes him who possesses one or the other, either good or evil. And from each let the appearance be subtracted. For unless you take away the reputation that truly belongs and replace it by the opposite, it may be said that you do not praise justice, but the appearance of justice. . . . Therefore show us not only that justice is worth more than injustice, but by what process justice itself, and by itself, makes him who possesses it good irrespective of whether manifest or hidden before the gods and before men.

Hide the appearance of the just even to the sight of God. Let the just man be abandoned even by God.

We find again this image of nakedness linked with that of death in Gorgias.

Gorgias, 523a

Hear this beautiful account. You may think it is a fable, but as for me, I think it is true. I shall tell it as a thing which really happened.

[Long, ago,] judgment of the living was rendered by the living. . . . Each one was judged on the day of his death. That is why the judgments were wrong. Pluto and the guardians of the Isles of the Blest came to tell Zeus that from both sides men arrived who were not worthy. Therefore Zeus said: Well, I'll put an end to that. At present wrong judgments are pronounced. That is so because those who are judged are clothed, in that they are living. But while many of those who are judged have criminal souls, they are dressed in beautiful bodies, in nobility and wealth, and when the judgment takes place, many witnesses accompany them to testify that they have lived righteously. All this makes an impression upon the judges. And moreover, the judges themselves are clothed. The eyes, the ears, the whole body act as a veil before their souls. Their own clothing and that of the accused blinds them. So, first of all, men should not know, as at present they do know, the hour of their death. Let Prometheus be told to put an end to that. Then let all come naked before their judges, which means they must be judged after they have died. The judge also should be naked, that is, he should be dead. By the soul alone he should weigh the naked soul of each one immediately after death, abandoned by all its kin, having left upon earth all earthly array so that the judgment may be right. I, having knowledge of these things before you, have appointed my sons to be judges . . . and when they shall be dead they shall judge in the open fields and at the parting where the two ways divide; one leads to the Isles of the blest, the other to Tartarus.

Death in my opinion is nothing else than the sundering of two things, the soul and the body, and when these are separated, each is in about the same condition as when the man was living. . . . If such a one was tall . . . so shall his corpse be, and likewise for the rest. . . . If his living body bore marks of the whip-lash, scars and welts and wounds, these are also visible upon his dead body. . . . It seems to me the same is true of the soul. All that is in the soul becomes apparent when the soul is naked, being stripped of its body, all natural dispositions and their effects which the soul suffers as a result of each worldly attachment. When it comes before the tribunal . . . [the judge] searches each soul without knowing to whom it belongs, then often, coming upon the soul of a great king, or a lesser king, or some other man of power, he sees that because of its perjuries and injustices, that soul is covered with stripes and scars which his acts have imprinted and that the whole is twisted by lies and vanities so that nothing in it is upright, being reared without truth. . . .

527e. Therefore believe me and follow me in this place which assures a happy life and a happy death when one arrives there. And allow whoever will to despise you for a senseless being, to insult you if he wants, and by Zeus learn to accept without wincing even that slap in the face of which you are always speaking; for nothing terrible can happen to you if you are truly good and noble, being practised in virtue.

In this context one finds:

1. Again the idea that judgment is nothing but the expression of what each one really *is*. Not an appreciation of what he has done, but a showing forth of what he is. Evil actions are reckoned only by the scars which they leave upon the soul. Here there is no application of a set rule, but a working out of strict necessity.

2. The image of nudity joined to that of death (the most ancient text? . . .). This double image is the purest mysticism.

There is no man, however wise or perceptive or just he may be, who is not influenced by the physical aspect and even more by the social position of people (if you believe . . .). An effect of the imagination. No one is unimpressed by dress. Victory or defeat, etc.

The truth is hidden by all that. *The truth is secret.* ('Your Father who seeth in secret'.) The truth is not revealed except in nakedness and that nakedness is death, which means the rupture of all those attachments which for each human being constitute the reason for living; those whom he loves, public esteem and possessions, material and moral, all that.

Plato does not say, but he implies, that to become wise, which exacts the knowledge of self, one must become, already in this life, naked and dead. The examination of conscience exacts this breaking of all the attachments which make up our reasons for living.

Moreover, he says explicitly in the *Phaedo*[1]:

Those who devote themselves as they should to the pursuit of wisdom, have no other goal than to die and to remain dead. . . . Death being nothing else than that state of the soul when it is separated from the body. . . . The soul of him who seeks wisdom scorns the body and flees it in order to be alone with itself. . . . It is only at this moment that we seem to possess our desires, that with which we claim we are in love: reason. Which means after our death, not while we are alive. For if it is impossible to have any pure knowledge so long as we are in the body, one of two things follows, either we never shall possess knowledge, or only after death; for then the soul will be itself, by itself, being far from the body, then and not before. And even while we live it seems clear that we shall be that much closer to wisdom as we refuse, beyond what is strictly necessary, to have dealings or union with the body, that we may not be filled by its nature, that we may purify ourselves of the flesh until God Himself comes to deliver us. . . . This purification consists in separating the soul as much as can be from the body, in setting it apart. And, having set it apart with itself alone, without the least

[1] 64a-67d.

contact with the body, in reassembling and in recollecting the soul, to make it dwell as far as possible, now and in the future, alone with itself and as freed as may be from the bonds of the flesh. . . . Finally, the detachment and the separation of the soul from the body, has for name: death.

It is almost certain that this double image of nakedness and death as symbol of spiritual salvation stems from the traditions of those secret cults which the ancients called 'The Mysteries'. See the Babylonian text of Ishtar in Hell. The Seven Doors: 'At each door one is stripped of something.' The meaning of the image of the door: 'Knock and it shall be opened unto you.' Osiris, and following him, Dionysus, died and was resuscitated. Descent into Hell as initiation.

The role of this double image in Christian spirituality: Death, St. Paul. Nakedness, St. John of the Cross and St. Francis.

If justice demands that during this life one be naked and dead, it is evident that this justice is impossible to human nature, and is supernatural.

It is first of all the flesh which prevents the soul from assimilation with God by justice, the flesh of which Plato, following the Orphics and the Pythagoreans, says: 'The body is the tomb of the soul.'[1]

Philolaus: [We know] by the testimony of ancient theologians and prophets it is because of chastisement that the soul is yoked to the body and buried in it as in a tomb.[2]

Numerous passages of Plato speak of the peril of the flesh.

Plato also took up another Pythagorean image comparing the sensitive and carnal part of the soul, the seat of desire, to an urn which for some men has its base pierced. For those who have received no light, the urn is pierced; they are thus continually busy pouring in all that they can without ever being able to fill it.[3]

---

[1] *Gorgias,* 493a; *Cratylus,* 400 c.   [2] Diels, 5th ed., I, p. 414.

[3] *Gorgias,* 494a.

But an even greater obstacle than the flesh is society. Upon this subject the image is terrible. This is an idea of first importance with Plato, one which runs through all his works, but not explicitly expressed, except in this passage, for reasons which the passage itself will explain. One never gives it enough importance.

> Do you believe as the vulgar do that only a few young men are corrupted by the sophists? Do you believe that this corruption, accomplished by a few sophists, a few private persons, is worth the trouble of mention? It is those who speak thus who are themselves the greatest sophists, it is they who administer mass education, they who form the character they desire in men and women, youths and old men.
>
> When is that? he asks. That, says Socrates, is when a great crowd is gathered in an assembly or tribunal, a theatre, or place of arms, or any assembly, and blames or praises words or actions with much tumult. They blame and praise to excess, they scream and clap their hands till the very rocks, and the place where they are assembled echoes, redoubling the tumult of blame or of applause.[1]

N.B. This seems to refer particularly to Athens, but one must transpose it. What follows shows that Plato meant it of all forms of social life without exception.

> In such a situation what would be the state of heart of the young man? What private education could make him steadfast enough not to be overwhelmed by these blames and these eulogies, not to be carried away by this current wherever it may be going? What could save him from declaring certain things beautiful, certain others shameful, according to the opinion of others? Would he not pursue the same things as they and become as they are.
>
> He would be powerfully forced to this, Socrates.
>
> And yet, said Socrates, I have not spoken of the greatest compulsion.
>
> Which? The action that these educators, these sophists, take against those whom they cannot persuade by words. Do you not know that he who will not be persuaded they punish with disgrace

[1] *Republic*, VI, 492.

and fines and death? Do you believe that any private sophistry or single individual could successfully stand up against that? No, certainly, and it would be great foolishness even to try.

For there is not, there never was, there never will be, any other teaching concerning morality than that of the multitude. At least no other human teaching. For concerning what is divine there must be exception. This must be well understood. Whatever is saved and becomes what it ought to be, so long as cities have their present structure, if one means to speak truly, must be considered saved by the effect of a predestination which comes from God.[1] ($\theta\epsilon o\hat{v}\ \mu o\hat{\iota}\rho a\nu$).

N.B. It is impossible to affirm more categorically that grace is the unique source of salvation, that salvation comes from God and not from man. The allusions to the court of law, the theatre, etc., which refer to Athenian life, might lead one to believe that this conception had no general bearing, but the words 'there is not, never was, nor ever will be' are proof to the contrary. Public opinion imposes itself under one form or another in every society without exception. There are two moralities, social morality and supernatural morality, and only those who are illumined by grace have access to the second.

The wisdom of Plato is not a philosophy, a search for God by means of human reason. Such a research was made as well as it can be made by Aristotle. Plato's wisdom is nothing but an orientation of the soul toward grace.

As for individuals who give paid lessons, the multitude calls them sophists and regards them as our rivals. But they only teach the opinions of the multitude, opinions which arise when a crowd is assembled. It is that which they call wisdom. Take for comparison a great, powerful beast; his keeper learns to know his angers and his desires, how best to approach him, from which side to touch him, at what moments and for what reasons he becomes irritable or gentle, what calls he customarily makes in such and such a humour, which words are apt to soothe or excite him. Suppose, having learned all such by practice over a period of time, the keeper calls

[1] VI, 492c.

that wisdom, and he makes a method of it, and uses it as subject-matter for his teaching. He knows nothing in reality of what among those opinions and desires is beautiful or ugly, good or evil, just or unjust. He uses those terms as they apply to the opinions of the great beast. Whatever pleases the animal he calls good, whatever annoys him he calls bad, and he has no other criterion. Things that are necessary he calls good and beautiful, for he is incapable of seeing or showing to others *to what degree the essence of the necessary is in reality different from the essence of good.*

Wouldn't this be a strange instructor? Well, he is exactly so who believes he can take for wisdom the aversions and the tastes of a crowd made up of dissenting elements, whether these be upon the subject of painting, or music, or politics. Thus if anyone has dealings with the multitude and communicates a poem or any other work of art or political idea, if he allows the multitude to become master outside the domain of necessary things, an iron necessity will force him to that which the multitude approves.[1]

This great beast, which is the social animal, is by every evidence the same as the beast of the Apocalypse.

This Platonic conception of society as the obstacle between man and God, obstacle which God alone can overcome, may also be compared with the words of the devil to Christ according to St. Luke:

He showed him all the kingdoms of the world in a moment of time. And the devil said unto him, All this power I will give thee, and the glory of them: for that is delivered unto me; and to whomsoever I will I give it.[2]

In parenthesis such a theory of society implies that society is essentially evil (in which Machiavelli is no more than a disciple of Plato, as were almost all the men of the Renaissance) and that the reform or tranformation of society can have no other reasonable object than to make it less evil. This is what Plato understood and his construction of an ideal city in the *Republic* is purely symbolic. There is frequent misunderstanding upon this subject.

[1] *Republic*, VI, 493a.   [2] St. Luke iv, 5-6.

Richelieu's remark. Machiavelli. Marxism, so far as it is true. Irreducible evil which one can only hope to limit. Rule: not to submit to society outside the domain of natural necessity.

It is difficult to grasp the import of this conception of Plato's because one does not realize to what degree one is the slave of social influences. By its very nature this slavery is almost always unconscious, and at those moments when it appears to the consciousness there is always the resource of lying to oneself in order to veil it.

Two remarks to throw a little light:

1. The opinions of the great beast are not necessarily contrary to the truth. They are formed by chance. It likes certain things that are bad and hates certain good things; but on the other hand there are some bad things which it hates, and some good things which it likes. But just where its opinions seem to accord with the truth, they are essentially foreign to the truth.

Example: If a person wants to steal but resists doing so, there is a great difference between resisting from obedience to the great beast or from obedience to God. The trouble is that one can easily tell oneself that one is obeying God and in reality be obeying the great beast. Because words can always be made to serve no matter what.

Thus the fact that upon a certain point one thinks or acts according to the truth in no way proves that upon this point one may not be a slave to the great beast.

All the virtues have their reflection in the morality of the great beast except humility, that key to the supernatural which is also mysterious, transcendent, indefinable and unrepresentable. (Egypt.)

2. In fact all that contributes to our education *is made up exclusively of things which at one or another epoch have been approved by the great beast.*

Racine. *Andromaque* and *Phèdre*. If instead he had begun with Phèdre. . . .

The historical facts: Those men whose names have come down

to us have gained fame by means of the great beast. Those whom it does not make famous continue unknown to their contemporaries and to all posterity.

Finally, notice that the blame of the great beast had the power to lead all the disciples of Christ, without exception, to abandon their master. As we are worth so much less than they, it is certain that the great beast has at least as much power over us without our realizing it (which is much worse) at every instant, even at this very moment. And that part of us which it has, God has not.

Granted that the grace necessarily emanates from God, of what does that grace consist, by what process is it accomplished, in what manner may a man receive it? Texts: *The Republic, Phaedrus, The Symposium.* Plato uses images. The fundamental idea of these images is that love is the disposition of the soul to which grace is given, which alone is able to receive grace, love and none other than love. Love of God is the root and foundation of Platonic philosophy.

Fundamental idea: Love, oriented toward itself, as object that is to say, perfection, makes contact with the only absolutely real reality. Protagoras said: 'Man is the measure of all things.' Plato replies: 'Nothing imperfect is the measure of anything.'[1] And: 'God is the measure of all things.'[2]

The one good is above justice and above all other virtues which we seek because of that part of good which is in them.

[1] *Republic*, VI, 504a.   [2] *Laws*, IV, 716c.

VIII

DIVINE LOVE IN CREATION[1]

PHERECYDES

(A Syrian who was perhaps the master of Pythagoras at the beginning of the sixth century B.C.)

Pherecydes said that Zeus transformed himself into Love at the moment of creating; for, in composing the order of the world out of contraries, he has brought it into harmony and love, and he has sown in all things the identity and the unity which spreads throughout the universe.

Timaeus, 28 a-b

All that is made comes of necessity from a maker. It is completely impossible that without a creator there should be a creation. If the artist looks at what is eternally interchanging, and when using that as a model, he reproduces the essence and meaning of it, perfect beauty is thereby of necessity accomplished. If he looks at what passes, if his model is transitory, what he makes is not beautiful.

These few lines comprehend a theory of artistic creation. There is no true beauty unless the work of art proceeds from a transcendent inspiration (the transcendent model simply signifies the veritable source of the inspiration). A work of art which is

---

[1] From *Les Intuitions Préchrétiennes*, pages 22-41.

inspired by sensual or psychological phenomena cannot be of the very first order. This verifies itself experimentally. One cannot imagine creation except by translating it into terms of human activity. But, whereas today we take as point of departure an activity such as that of a clockmaker, which leads into absurdities from the moment we make the substitution, Plato chose an activity which, although human, had already something of the supernatural. Moreover, one can verify the legitimacy of this analogy. One can never find enough visible finality in the world to prove that it is analogous to an object made with a view to a certain end. It is even manifest that this is not the case. Yet the analogy between the world and a work of art has its experimental verification in the very feeling itself of the beauty of the world, for the beautiful is the only source of the sense of beauty. This verification is valid only for those who have experienced that feeling, but those who have never felt it, and who are doubtless very rare, cannot perhaps be brought to God by any path. In comparing the world to a work of art, it is not only the act of creation but Providence itself which is found to be assimilated in the artistic inspiration. That is to say that in the world, as in the work of art, there is completion without any imaginable end. All human creations are adjustments of means in view of determinate ends, except the work of art, in which there is adjustment of means, where obviously there is completion, but where one cannot conceive of an end. In a sense the end is nothing but the very arrangement, the assembling itself of the means employed; in another sense the end is completely transcendent. Exactly the same is true of the universe and of the course of the universe, of which the end is eminently transcendent and not representable, since that end is God Himself. Art is thus the unique legitimate term of comparison. Moreover, this comparison alone leads to love. One can use a watch without loving the watchmaker, but one cannot listen with attention to a faultlessly beautiful song without love for the composer of the song and for the singer. In the same way the watchmaker does not need love to make a watch, whereas artistic creation (that sort which is not demonic but simply human) is nothing but love.

Timaeus

28c. The creator and father of this universe is found only by toil and it is not possible for the man who finds Him to reveal Him to all men. Therefore let us examine again which of the two models this carpenter has chosen to execute, the one identical with itself and so remains, or that which passes? If this world is beautiful, if the artist is good, obviously he has looked towards the eternal; in the other case, of which it is blasphemous even to speak, towards the one that passes. It is indeed entirely manifest that he looked towards the eternal. For the one (world) is the most beautiful of works, and the other (God) the most perfect of causes. Therefore this world of becoming has been executed in the likeness of that unchangeable being who is possessed of intelligence and reason.

29d. Let us now determine for what reason the composer composed this becoming and this universe. He was good, and, in him who is good, never in any case, never in any manner, was envy found. Being without envy, he wanted all things to be made as much as possible like himself. . . . God willed that all things should be good and that nothing should be deprived of that value which is its own.

30b. Let us admit that this world is a living being who has a soul, that it is a spiritual being and that in verity it has been engendered such by the Providence of God.

30c. This being admitted, it must next be disclosed which is the one among living creatures in whose likeness the composer has composed the world. It cannot be anything which is essentially incomplete. That would be unworthy, for whatever resembles imperfection cannot be beautiful. To him whose being comprises all living creatures, considered individually and in their species as parts, this world bears the greatest resemblance. This being contains in himself all living spirits, just as the world comprehends in itself ourselves and all visible creatures. For God wanted the world to resemble completely that one among spiritual beings who is absolutely beautiful, absolutely perfect in every way; and He composed a living visible being, unique, having within Himself all living beings who are related to Him by nature. . . . In order that by unity, the world should be like the absolutely perfect being. For this reason, the creator did not create two worlds, or numberless worlds; for there has been born, there exists, there shall exist, a single heaven which is this one, who is the only begotten son.

Plato, when he speaks of the world, or heaven, means essentially the Soul of the World; just as when we call a friend by his name we have in mind his soul and not his body. This being which Plato calls the Soul of the World is the unique Son of God; Plato says, 'monogenes' like St. John. The visible world is his body. That does not imply pantheism; he is not in the visible world just as our soul is not in our body. Plato says this explicitly elsewhere. The Soul of the World is infinitely more vast than matter, contains matter and envelopes it from all parts (34b). It was begotten before the visible world, before time, consequently from all eternity (34c). The Soul of the World commands the material world as the master commands the slave. It contains in itself the substance of God united to the principle of matter.

The model in whose likeness the Soul of the World is engendered is a living spiritual being, or a living spirit. It is therefore a person. This is the spirit which is absolutely perfect in every way. He is therefore God. There are then three divine persons, the Father, the Only Son, and the Model. To understand that the third can be named the Model, one must go back to the comparison at the beginning of *Timaeus*, the comparison with artistic creation. The artist of the very first order works after a transcendent model, which he does not represent, which is only for him the supernatural source of his inspiration. As soon as one replaces model by the word inspiration, the appropriateness of this image when applied to the Holy Spirit becomes evident. Even in conceiving the comparison in its coarsest form, when a painter makes a portrait, the model is the link between the artist and the picture.

34b.   The Soul [i.e. of the World] he places in the centre; he spreads it out across the whole and even beyond the corporeal universe, enveloping it, and, by rolling it in a circle in a circular heaven, he establishes it one, unique, solitary, capable by its own virtue of being its own companion, having need of nothing other than itself, known and loved sufficiently itself by itself. In this manner he begets this happy God: the world.

34c.   He has established the Soul [of the World] first among members of the body in age as in dignity, and has given it to the body as a mistress and a sovereign to be obeyed.

36b.   This whole composition he split in two by its length, then he applied the parts one upon the other, by the middle as in the letter X; he bent them in a circle and attached one to the other opposite the point of crossing, then he enveloped them in the movement which turns in an identical manner upon the same centre.

This composition is the substance of the Soul of the World, made of a synthesis of the divine substance itself and of the principle of matter.

A while ago Plato said that the Soul of the World, the only son, is a happy God, known and loved Himself by Himself. In other words, He has in Himself the blessed life of the Trinity. But here Plato shows that same God torn apart. It is the involvement with space and time which constitutes this cleavage, which is already a sort of Passion. St. John also, in the Apocalypse (xiii, 8), speaks of the 'Lamb slain from the foundation of the world.' The two halves of the Soul of the World are crossed, one upon the other; the cross is oblique, but all the same it is a sort of cross. But opposite to that crossing point the two halves are joined and welded, and the whole is enveloped by the circular movement, a movement which changes nothing, which curls upon itself; the perfect image of the eternal and blessed act which is the life of the Trinity.

The image of the two circles which Plato uses represents the equator, which determines the daily movement of the field of fixed stars, and that of the ecliptic, which determines the annual movement of the sun. The point where the two circles cross marks the equinox of spring (the fact that among the ancients the year began in many countries in the spring, never, I think, in autumn, outrules the supposition that it could be a question of the autumnal equinox.) The position of the equinox of spring, in Plato's time, was in the constellation of the Ram, the sun in the Easter position and the moon at the opposite equinoctial point. If people read Plato in the same state of mind as they read the Old Testament, they would perhaps see a prophecy in these lines. By this prodigious combination of symbols, Plato shows us in the heavens, and in the course of days, and of seasons, an image at once of the Trinity and of the cross.

> 36d. When the composer had realized his whole conception of the Soul [of the World], he next spread throughout the interior the whole corporeal universe and he adjusted the two by making the centres meet. He spread the Soul from the centre throughout, even to the confines of heaven, and he enveloped the whole sphere of heaven outside. The Soul, turning upon itself, began the divine beginning of an inextinguishable and wise life for the totality of time. And the visible body of the heavens was born; and the invisible Soul, which shares in proportion and in harmony, was born as the perfection of begotten spirits, begotten of the perfection of eternal spirits.

One should not be misled by these two plurals. Their *raison d'être* is purely grammatical. They are brought in by superlatives and do not prevent the Father and the Son being unique.

This passage shows that in the myth from the *Phaedrus*, when Zeus passes to the other side of heaven to partake of his repast, it is his only son whom he eats, the reference here being to the transposition of God in the communion. The beatified souls also eat him.

The participation of the Soul of the World in proportion and in harmony should not be understood only as the ordering function of the Word. It should be understood in a much more profound sense. Proportion and harmony are synonyms. Proportion is the bond established between two numbers by a mean proportional; thus 3 establishes a proportion between 1 and 9, that is $\frac{1}{3} = \frac{3}{9}$. Harmony is defined by the Pythagoreans as the unity of contraries. The first couple of contraries is God and the creature. The Son is the unity of these contraries, the geometrical mean which establishes a proportion between them: He is the mediator.

37d.   The Model, having eternal life, has tried to give as much as possible of that life to the universe also. Now the nature of the living [Model], being eternal, could not be absolutely given to that which is begotten. So he conceived the idea of creating a mobile image of eternity. At the same time as he established the order of heaven, he created a thing which, revolving by the law of number, is the eternal image of that eternity which is fixed in unity. That image is what we call time.

38a.   The past and the future appeared as the forms of time which imitate eternity by revolving according to the law of number.

38c.   So, according to God's order and thought concerning the creation of time, to which end time was made, the sun and the moon and the five other stars which are called planets, appeared. Their function being the measurement and the preservation of the numbers of time:

39b.   So that the sun might be from all sides as visible as possible, and that the living might have part in number, all those at least for whom such was appropriate.

47b.   Contemplation of the circular movements of intelligence in the heavens should serve as guide for the circular translations of thought in ourselves which are related to them. But the heavenly movements are untroubled while ours are disturbed; we should be instructed by this and take part in the essential rectitude of heavenly proportions. By the imitation of God's circular motions, which are absolutely without error, we should make our own errant motions stable.

Thus the Word is a model for man to imitate. Not in this case the Word incarnate in a human being, but the Word as the orderer of the world, so far as incarnate in the universe as a whole. Here is the source of the idea of microcosm and of macrocosm which so haunted the Middle Ages. Its profundity is almost impenetrable. The symbol of the circular movement is the key to it. We must force this insatiable desire in us, which is always turned outward and which has an imaginary future for its domain, to turn back upon itself and to focus upon the present. The movements of the celestial bodies which divide our life into days, months and years are our model in this regard, because their rotations are so regular that for them the future in no way differs from the past. By contemplating this equivalence of the future and the past we pierce through time right to eternity, and being delivered from desire oriented toward the future, we are delivered also from the imagination which accompanies it and is the unique source of error and of untruth. We share in the rectitude of proportions in which there is nothing arbitrary, therefore no field open to the play of the imagination. But doubtless this idea of proportion also evokes the Incarnation.

47e. Now what happens by necessity must also be added to this exposition. For the creation of this world took place by a combination composed partly of necessity and partly of mind. But the mind reigns over necessity by persuasion. Mind persuades necessity tc move the greater part of created things toward improvement. It is in this manner, according to this law, by means of a necessity vanquished by a wise persuasion, it is thus that from the beginning this universe was created.

These lines recall the Chinese conception of God's non-aggressive action, which, moreover, is found again in many Christian texts; also the passages from the *Symposium* on the

gentleness of Love, who does no violence, who is obeyed voluntarily; also these lines from Aeschylus:

> Zeus strikes down ruined mortals
> from their hopes lofty as towers,
> but he arms himself with no violence.
> All that is divine is without effort.
> Seated above, his wisdom knows
> from there how to accomplish all things,
> from his pure throne.
>
> (*Suppliants*, vv. 95 sqq.)

God does no violence to secondary causes in the accomplishment of his ends. He accomplishes them all through the inflexible
mechanism of necessity without warping a single wheel. His
wisdom remains above (and when it descends, it does so, as we
know, with a like discretion). Each phenomenon has two causes,
of which one is its cause according to the mechanism of nature,
that is, natural law, the second cause is in the providential ordering
of the world, and it never is permissible to make use of the one as
an explanation upon the plane to which the other belongs.

This aspect of the order of the world should also be imitated
by us. Once a certain threshold is crossed, the supernatural part
of the soul reigns over the natural part not by violence but by
persuasion, not by will but by desire.

90a. It must be understood concerning that part of the soul to
which the sovereignty in us belongs, that this is a divine being,
God-given to each one of us. I affirm that this being inhabits the
summit of our body, and that by his kinship with heaven he lifts us
above the earthly because we are not an earthly but a heavenly plant.
One may correctly speak thus. For from the place, where originally
the birth of the soul germinated, this divine being holds the head
suspended, which is our root, and thus he maintains the body upright.

90c. [One must] always be at the service of this divine being;
maintaining that station which is appropriate for the divine being
who dwells within us.

97

There is never but one manner to serve a being, that is to give it the food and the movement which it needs. The movements which are natural to the divine being in us are the thoughts and the circular movements of the universe. Each one should apply himself to follow these, to correct the circular movements in his head relative to things which pass and those that are corrupt, by learning the harmonies of the circular movements of the universe. The contemplative being must be brought, as his original nature demands, to a resemblance of what is contemplated. Once this resemblance is attained, he possesses the accomplishment of the perfect life proposed to men by the gods for their present and future existence.

In speaking of the circular motions of the universe, Plato is thinking not only of the cycles of the day, the month and the year but also of the ideas which unite them in his system of symbols, that is the *Same* and the *Other*; in other words, identity and diversity, unity and multiplicity, absolute and relative, pure good and good mixed with evil, spiritual and perceptible, supernatural and natural. The stars turn only parallel to the equator, the sun turns parallel at once to the equator and to the ecliptic. Similarly, in these contrary pairs, which make but one, the second term is not symmetrical with the first but subordinate, even while being opposed to it. All possible events come to fit themselves into the framework constituted by the two combined movements of the celestial sphere and of the sun, the frame of days distributed in seasons throughout the year is there without ever in any way being able to disturb it. Such a disturbance is not even thinkable. Likewise the pleasures and the pains, the fears and the desires, even the most violent, must fit in us without causing the least disturbance in the established relations of our soul between the part turned toward this world and the part that is turned toward the other world. This relationship must be such that it perpetually sheds a light of eternity over the course of minutes, no matter what may be the events that come to fill those minutes.

The image of man as a plant whose root penetrates heaven is

98

linked in the *Timaeus* to a theory of chastity, which Plato has concealed by separating it in several parts so that I do not know whether anyone has seen it there. This plant is sprinkled by celestial water, a divine semen, which enters the head. In that man who continually exercises the spiritual and the intellectual part of himself, by contemplating and by imitating the order of the world, in him the whole contents of the head, including the divine semen, is propelled by circular movements like those which govern the rotation of the heavens, the stars and the sun. This divine semen is what Plato calls the divine being lodged with us, in us, and whom we must serve. But in the man or the woman who leaves these highest faculties of the soul inert, the circular movements in the head are disturbed or arrested. Then the divine semen descends the length of the vertebral column and becomes carnal desire. It is still an independent being inhabiting the man, but now a demonic being who hears no reason and wants to dominate all by violence. It is thus that Plato speaks of it at the end of the *Timaeus*.

To express it otherwise, instead of seeing love of God as a sublimated form of carnal desire, as many people in our wretched epoch do, Plato thinks that carnal desire is a corruption, a degradation, of love of God. And, although it is very difficult to interpret certain of these images, it is certain that he conceived this relationship as a truth not only spiritual but biological as well. He evidently thought that the glands of those who love God do not function in the same manner as the glands of those who do not. The love of God being, of course, the cause and not the effect of this difference.

This conception is inspired by the religion of the Mysteries; for the link between chastity and love of God is the central idea in the *Hippolytus* of Euripides, a tragedy of Eleusinian and Orphic inspiration. (Be it said in passing that there has not been to my knowledge during the last twenty centuries in the theatre of the different countries of Europe any other tragedy which has this idea for its central theme.)

To understand the range of meaning which Plato comprised under the symbolism of circular motion it should be noted that this motion is the perfect combination of whole number and continuity. The moving point passes from one point to the next without any break in continuity, as it would in passing along a straight line. But at the same time if one fixes one's attention on any one point of the circumference, the describing point must necessarily pass over it an integral number of times, Circular motion is thus an image of that unison of the limited and the limitless of which Plato says in *Philebus* that it is the key of all knowledge and the gift to mortals from Prometheus. It is moreover strictly true that this union constitutes our idea of time, and that time reflects the circular movement of the astral bodies. Time is continuity, but we count the days and the years by whole numbers. To recognize that this is not a theme for meditation by intellectuals but a thing absolutely essential for all men, it is sufficient to remember that one of the most horrible of tortures consists in putting a man in a dungeon completely dark, or alternatively in a cell always lighted by electricity, without ever telling him the date or the hour. If one only thinks of that enough, one will find a profound joy in the simple succession of days. Such considerations being surely no less cogent in the time of St. Benedict; the monastic rules have among other purposes that of making the circular character of time more clearly felt. Herein is also the secret of the virtue of music.

The Pythagoreans said, not the union of the limited and the limitless, but what is much more beautiful: the union of that which limits and the non-limited. That which limits is God. God who says to the sea: Hitherto shalt thou come, but no further. . . . That which is unlimited has no existence except in receiving a limit from outside. All that exists here below is similarly constituted; not only all material realities but all the psychological realities in ourselves and in others as well. So in this world there are none but finite joys and sorrows. The infinite joys and sorrows which we think of as existing in this world, and which furthermore we necessarily situate in the future, are absolutely imaginary. The desire for infinite good which dwells at every moment in all men, even the most degraded, has its objective outside this world, and the privation of this good is the only ill not subject to limitation. To place the knowledge of this truth at the centre of the soul, in a manner whereby all the movements of the soul are ordered in relation to it, is to imitate the order of the world. For thus the content of the soul is unlimited, that is to say, absolutely all that is contained in its natural part receives a limit imprinted from outside by God present within the soul. It is still full of the same naturally disordered pleasures and pains, fears and desires, just as in the world of nature there are very hot summers and freezing winters, floods and droughts, but all these are nevertheless continually bound up with, and in submission to, an absolutely unalterable order.

The contemplation of relationships of arithmetical and geometric quantity is very useful in achieving this, as all that partakes of quantity in whatever manner clearly shows. This means that not only matter and space but all that is in time and is susceptible to degree is pitilessly and by the chains of necessity subordinated to limit.

This contemplation attains its whole fruit when the incomprehensible ordering of these relationships, and the marvellous concordances which one finds in them, make one feel that the very enslavement, which is necessity, or law, upon the plane of the intelligence, is beauty upon the plane immediately above, and is obedience in relation to God.

When one has understood to the depths of the soul that necessity is only one of the faces of beauty, the other being the good, then all that makes necessity felt, contradictions, sorrows, ills, obstacles, become a further reason for loving. Among the people there is a saying that when an apprentice hurts himself, it is the craft entering into the body.

Beauty itself is the Son of God. For he is the image of the Father, and the beautiful is the image of the good.

The end of the book of Job, and the first verses spoken by Prometheus in Aeschylus' tragedy, indicate a mysterious bond between suffering and the revelation of the beauty of the world.

> 'O divine heaven, swift wings of wind,
> O rivers and their sources, O seas and
> numberless smiling waves, and thou,
>   mother of all, earth,
> and that one who sees all, disk of the sun,
>   I call upon you
> to see in me what sufferings the gods bring
>   to a god.'
>
> (*Prometheus*, vv. 88 sqq.)

Of course, joy is also a manner in which beauty enters into us, even the coarsest of joys, so long as they are innocent.

There are a few lines from Plato's *Symposium* upon the beauty of the sciences, as one of the highest rungs on the way which leads to Beauty itself, that is, toward the Image of God. Upon the employment of sorrow and of joy there is one indication in *Philebus*. These two are quoted further on.

The essential idea of the *Timaeus* is that the foundation, the substance of this universe wherein we live, is love. It has been created by love and its beauty is the reflection and the irrefutable sign of this divine love, as the beauty of a perfect statue, of a perfect song, is the reflection of supernatural love which fills the soul of a truly inspired artist.

Moreover, the dream of every sculptor to make a statue having a soul and real flesh, is a dream realized by God. He has given a soul to his statue and that soul is identical with himself.

When one sees a truly beautiful human being, which is very rare, or when one hears the song of a truly beautiful voice, one cannot deny the belief that behind that beauty which speaks to the senses there is a soul made of the purest love. Very often this is false, and such errors often cause great misfortunes. But for the universe it is true. The beauty of the world speaks to us of the

Love which is its soul, as the features of a human face which did not lie might be perfectly beautiful.

There are unfortunately many moments, and even long periods of time, when we are not sensitive to the beauty of the world because a screen comes between it and ourselves. That screen may be men and their wretched fabrications, or it may be the ugliness of our own soul. But we can always know that beauty exists, and know that all that we touch, see and hear is the very flesh and the very voice of absolute Love.

Once again, there is in this conception no hint of pantheism, for such a soul is not in this body but contains it, penetrates it, envelops it upon all sides, being itself outside space and time; being not entirely distinct from these but governing them. And this soul allows itself to be perceived by us through our sense of beauty, as an infant finds in its mother's smile, in an inflection of her voice, the revelation of the love of which itself is the object.

It would be an error to believe that a sensitivity to beauty is the privilege of a small number of cultivated people. On the contrary, beauty is the only value that is universally recognized. Among the people the term beautiful, or synonymous terms, are constantly employed to praise not only a town, or a country, but even the most unexpected things, for example a machine. The general bad taste is responsible for the fact that men, cultivated or not, often apply these terms very mistakenly, but that is another question. The essential is that the word beauty speaks to all hearts.

The second idea in the *Timaeus* is that this world, at the same time as it is the mirror of this Love which is God himself, is also the model which we must imitate. For we also have originally been, and must again become, images of God. We can only do this by the imitation of the perfect Image which is the only Son of God who thinks the order of the world.

This idea of the order of the world as object of contemplation and of imitation can alone make the supernatural destination of science understood. Nothing is more important today, seeing the current prestige of science and the place which it holds even in the minds of almost illiterate people. Science in all its branches, from mathematics to sociology, has the order of the world for object. This is only seen under the aspect of necessity, all consideration of appropriateness or of purpose having to be rigorously excluded, with the exception of the very notion of universal order itself. The more rigorous, precise, demonstrative, strictly scientific science is, the more the essentially providential character of the order of the world becomes manifest. What we call the design or designs, the plan or plans, of Providence, are only imaginings invented by ourselves. What is authentically providential, what is Providence itself, is this very order of the world itself, the stuff of which it is woven, the woof of all events, and which, beneath one of its aspects, is the pitiless and blind mechanism of necessity. Because, once and for all, necessity has been vanquished by the wise persuasion of Love. This wise persuasion is Providence. This submission without constraint on the part of necessity to loving wisdom is beauty. Beauty excludes selfish ends. When, in a poem, one can explain that such a word has been placed where it is by the poet to produce such and such an effect, for instance a rich rhyme, an alliteration, a certain image, and so on, the poem is second-rate. Of a perfect poem one can say only that each word is in the place where it is absolutely appropriate to be. Likewise for all beings (including oneself), for all things, for all happenings which insert themselves into the course of time. When again, after a long absence, we see an ardently loved human being, and he speaks to us, each word is infinitely precious, not because of its significance but because the presence of him whom we love makes itself understood in each syllable. Even if, by chance, we are suffering at the moment from such a violent headache that each sound is painful, the voice which brings us this presence is no less dear and precious on account of the pain it causes. Likewise, he who loves God has no need to picture to himself such and such a good which may possibly result from an event which has taken place. Every event that takes place is a syllable pronounced by the voice of Love himself.

It is because Providence governs the world, as inspiration governs the material of a work of art, that it is also a source of inspiration to us. The idea of a table in the mind of a cabinetmaker produces a table and nothing more. But the work of art which is the effect of the artist's inspiration is a source of inspiration to those who contemplate it. Through the work of art, the love which is in the artist begets a like love in other souls. So does absolute Love throughout the universe.

This transcendent conception of Providence is the essential teaching of the *Timaeus*. A teaching of such depth that I cannot believe it could have come down to the human mind except by revelation.

IX

THE 'SYMPOSIUM' OF PLATO[1]

THE SUBJECT of the *Symposium* is Love, that is to say the divinity who bears that name. Aristophanes' myth, of incontestably Orphic inspiration, shows Love, contained like the germ of the chicken in the egg of the World, which hatches with golden wings, indicating that Love is the same thing as the Soul of the World. It is therefore the Son of God. It is moreover significant that Aristophanes should be one of the orators of the *Symposium*; his dissertation is indeed one of the most beautiful; and yet Plato had the gravest motives for resenting him because of his cruel mockeries and injustices toward Socrates which were perhaps not without influence upon the verdict of the trial. If, nevertheless, Plato put Aristophanes in this work, one may legitimately suppose that it is precisely on account of these verses concerning Love and the egg of the World. On the other hand, if one reads the *Prometheus* of Aeschylus and the *Symposium* in the Greek, one immediately after the other, one finds in Plato's text a certain number of words which seem clearly to constitute allusions to Aeschylus' tragedy, and that notably in the discourse of the tragic poet Agathon. Finally, the setting itself of this dialogue, this banquet where there is hardly a question of food, but where there is ceaselessly a question of wine, the arrival of a drunken Alcibiades at the end, the discourse where, in a long comparison,

[1] From *Les Intuitions Préchrétiennes*, pages 41-71.

he likens Socrates to Silenus, that is, to an attendant of Dionysus, all this is evidently designed for placing the work under the protection of Dionysus. And Dionysus is the same god as Osiris, the god whose passion was celebrated, the judge and saviour of souls, the Lord of the truth.

DISCOURSE OF ERYXIMACHUS THE PHYSICIAN

186b. This great and marvellous God holds sway over all, in things human and in those which are divine.

186d. The opposed and contrary things are, the cold and the hot, the bitter and the sweet, the dry and the humid, and so on. It is after having learned how to bring love and concord to these elements that our ancestor Asclepius constituted our art. Thus all medicine is directed by the God of Love, as also are gymnastics and agriculture. For music, the same reconciliation of opposites is entirely manifest ... starting with what is at first divergent, the high and the low pitch, when these are subsequently brought into proportion, harmony is produced by the art of music. For harmony is like an accord of voices, and the agreement of voices is a certain proportion.

187b. Similarly, rhythm is produced from the slow and the rapid, first divergent, then brought into proportion.

187c. In these contraries music, as in other contraries medicine, implants proportion, thus creating love and mutual accord; and music is the science of love in the domain of harmony and of rhythm.

188b. And again the whole business of sacrifices and prophetic inspiration—which constitute the mutual association of gods and men—are concerned with nothing else than the security and the health of all that belongs to Love. For every impiety ensues when one does not try to please Love, the god of order, when one does not honour him, when one does not venerate him in every action; but pleases the other, the love of disorder. . . . The work assigned to prophetic inspiration is to watch over and to heal the loves. Prophecy is the worker of friendship between the gods and men by understanding human loves in their relationship with justice and impiety.

Love, the orderer, is divine Love. The love of disorder is demoniac love.

188d.   The love which has its perfection in the good along with self-restraint and justice possesses the supreme power among us, and among the Gods, and it prepares complete felicity for us in making us capable of fellowship and friendship among each other and among those who are worth more than ourselves: the Gods.

DISSERTATION OF ARISTOPHANES

189d.   Of all the Gods, Love is the greatest friend of men, their defender and the physician of those ills whose healing would be the supreme felicity for the human species.

This comparison between Love and a physician, a comparison which Christ in the Gospels applies to His mission, here concerns, as it did for Christ, the healing of original sin. Original sin is that illness whose cure would constitute the supreme felicity for man. For immediately after these lines in Plato's text there follows a story of the felicity of primitive man, of his sin, and his chastisement. This story needs to be interpreted.

Long ago man was a complete being. He had two faces, four legs and was capable of circular movements. He was guilty of pride and attempted to climb up to heaven (this recalls the Tower of Babel, but also the sin of Adam and Eve who wanted to be like God). Zeus wanted to punish these men, but without going so far as to destroy them, for in that case the honours and the praise that men gave to the gods would have disappeared.

This is also the same reason which, in the Eleusinian hymn to Demeter, influences Zeus to concede to Demeter when she threatens to stop the growth of the wheat, thereby causing men to die of hunger. It recalls the covenant which God makes in Genesis ix, 9-12 after the first sacrifice of Noah, to spare men henceforth. It is thus clearly indicated that if man, despite his mediocrity and his insolence, is allowed to live, that is solely because God wants to be loved by him. It is only in this sacrifice that man finds his purpose. God allows man existence so that man may have the possibility of renouncing it out of love for God.

Zeus, wishing to chastise man without destroying him, cuts him in two. The ancients had a frequent custom of cutting a ring, or a coin, or any other object in two and of giving one half to a friend or a guest. These halves were preserved by each side from generation to generation, permitting the descendants of the two friends to recognize each other after centuries.

Such a sign of recognition was called a symbol. That is the primitive sense of the word. In this sense, Plato says, each one of us is not a man, but the symbol of a man, and seeks the corresponding symbol, the other half. This quest is Love. Love in us is therefore the feeling of our radical insufficiency in consequence of sin, and the desire, coming from the very sources of our being, to be reintegrated into the state of completion. Love is thus the right physician for our original illness. We need not ask ourselves how to have love, it is in us from birth to death, imperious as hunger. We need only to know in what direction to direct it.

Carnal desire is a degraded form of this hunger for completeness. This form appears among men and women who are each half of an androgyne, it does not appear among those who are halves of completely masculine or feminine beings. This might lead one to believe in a distinction of the sexes in the original state, but as Plato also says that in that original state there was no union of the sexes, that procreation was operated differently, it is clear that he pictures that state as being without distinction of sex, and that when he divides those beings having two faces and four legs into three classes, males, females and androgynes, this is simply a manner of speaking. He calls those who incline to the basest desire the issue of androgynes. This is explicitly said: 'Men who are halves of what we have named androgynes love women, and the greater part of adulterers issue from this species. Likewise among women, those who love men and are adulteresses are born of this species' (191e). In speaking of men who are halves of complete males, he designates them simply as those who are capable of chastity. That also is explicitly said: 'None could believe that it is for the practice of carnal pleasures that they so ardently rejoice in being together.' And the same for the women.

This whole discourse of Aristophanes is obscure, of an evidently wilful obscurity. But the essential idea is manifestly this. Our vocation is unity. Our affliction is to be in a state of duality, an affliction due to an original contamination of pride and of injustice. The division of the sexes is only a sensible image of that state of duality which is our essential defect, and carnal union is the deceitful appearance of a remedy. But the desire to escape from the state of duality is the sign of Love in us, and only the god of Love can bring us back from that duality to the unity which is our sovereign good. What is that unity? It evidently is not a question of the union of two human beings. That duality which is our affliction is the division by which he who loves is other than that which is loved, he who knows is other than that which is known, the material of the action other than the one who acts, it is the separation of the subject and the object. Unity is that state wherein the subject and the object are one single and the same thing, the state of him who knows himself and who loves himself. But only God is thus, and we cannot become thus except by assimilation in God, which the love of God accomplishes.

191d. Each of us then is the 'symbol' of a man who has been split in two in the manner of a fish and each one is perpetually searching for the 'symbol' which belongs to him.

192c. And those who pass their whole lives together are the very ones who could not tell what they want of each other. For none could believe it to be for the sake of carnal pleasure that they have such intense joy in being together, rather it is manifest that the soul of each one longs for another thing which it is unable to name, and expresses this desire as by oracles and enigmas.

192d. If Hephaestus should ask . . .
Is this your desire, to become absolutely one and the same each

with the other, to the extent of not being separated day or night? If this is what you desire, I am willing to weld and to unite you in a single being, in such a way that from being two you shall become one, and that all your life. being one, you shall lead a common existence. And when you die, there below in that other world also, instead of two, you shall be but one in death. . . . We know well that upon hearing such a proposal neither would refuse, it would be manifest to each that he desires nothing else, he would think he has by miracle just heard the expression of the very thing he has long desired, which is to be united and welded to the one he loves and instead of being two, to become one. The reason of this is that our primitive nature was such: we have been whole beings. The desire and the quest for integrity has love for its name. And originally, I affirm it, we were a unity. Now, because of our injustice, we have been divided by God.

193a. Every man should encourage every other to piety toward the gods. . . .

193b. To the end that we may receive those blessings for the conquest of which Love is our guide and our leader. Let no one disobey him. All those disobey him who are hateful to the gods. For if we become friends with God, and if we are reconciled with him, we shall each receive the object of our loves. . . .

193c. I say that for all men and all women, it is by this means that our species would become blessed, if we would realize our love, if each would obtain the object of his love, it is by returning to our primitive state. If herein is the supreme good, it necessarily follows that among the things of this world the greatest good is that which most nearly approaches that state; in which each one shall receive that object of love which is spiritually essential to him. To praise the God who works that in us, it is right that we should sing to Love, who is at this moment the most useful of all in guiding us toward our own nature, and who for the future gives us the fullness of hope, the hope that if we show piety towards the gods, He will establish us in our primitive state, will heal us and keep us in blessedness.

It appears in these lines that not only carnal love but also platonic love and friendship, although of a higher order, are only images of that integrity, that primitive unity, to which man aspires from the depth of his soul. In fact, Hephaestus never addresses anyone in the language which Plato pretends for a moment to put in his mouth. It is not with a man that a man can be thus indissolubly united. This can only be with God. It is only in becoming again the friend of God that man can hope to receive, in the other world, after death, the unity, the integrity, which he needs.

Plato never tells all in these myths. It is not arbitrary to extend them. It would be much more arbitrary not to extend them. In this one Plato says that after the complete man has been cut in two, the front of the body corresponds to the incision, Zeus ordered Apollo to change the face from the side to the front, that is to say the organs of the senses, and the sexual organs. It is natural to imagine, in extending the metaphor, that in the return to the state of integrity all that would somehow become internal to the complete being. Otherwise expressed, the complete being is, as Plato says of the Soul of the World in the *Timaeus*, 'known and sufficiently loved himself by himself' at once subject and object. It is just this state which Plato points to when he says that he who loves will make but one with him who is loved, this unique being must be at once the subject and the object, otherwise love would disappear and there would be no felicity. Granted that such integrity belongs only to God, man may have part in it only by the union of love with God. Plato's myth points out that the integrity to which man arrives by the grace of Love in blessed Eternity is of a superior order to that which he lost by sin, that sin is therefore a 'happy fault', just as it is called in the Catholic liturgy, *felix culpa*.

It is impossible to emphasize more clearly than Plato does here that the God whom he names Love is a god of redemption.

The analogies between Love and Prometheus begin to appear in this discourse of Aristophanes. First by the epithet 'the greatest friend of men'. Aeschylus in his tragedy constantly says of Prometheus that he is the friend of men, that he has loved mortals too much, even that he has venerated them too much (see citations further on). It is impossible to show oneself more the friend of man than Prometheus did. This superlative applied to Love would be entirely unjust if the two names did not belong to the same God. Another analogy appears in the link between Love and the anger of Zeus against men. In Aristophanes' speech, Zeus considers completely exterminating humanity, but refrains from it in order not at the same time to abolish religion itself; instead of that he inflicts upon humanity an ill of which Love is the physician. In the tragedy of Aeschylus, Zeus wants to exterminate humanity but does not do so because Prometheus prevents him, it is not said by what means; then, instead of punishing humanity, Zesu makes Prometheus suffer. The two myths are far from identical but still not without resemblance. For the rest one must not regard these myths and all those which bear a resemblance to them as factual accounts but as symbols, in such a way that different myths may correspond to the same truth seen from different angles.

DISCOURSE OF THE TRAGIC POET AGATHON

195a. I affirm that of all the Gods, Love is the most joyful, the most beautiful and the most perfect.

Therefore Love is the equal of Zeus. Notice that although these superlatives are relative, they must be understood as absolute superlatives, for in Plato there is no childish polytheism.

195d. He walks not upon what is hard but upon what is tender . . . for he establishes his habitation in the hearts and the souls of gods and of men, and not in all the souls; if he encounters one whose character is hard, he turns away toward one whose character is tender, and there he establishes himself. . . . He is thus very young and very delicate, moreover his substance is fluid. For otherwise he would be incapable of insinuating himself everywhere through the whole soul and he could not pass unseen as he does, at first, when he enters and when he leaves, if he were made of a hard material. A great proof that he has proportion and fluidity is the beauty of his form, an incomparable beauty according to universal opinion, for there is perpetual war between ugliness and Love. The beauty of his complexion is indicated by his habitual habitation among the flowers, for Love does not come to rest upon a body or upon a soul or upon any other thing which is without flower, which has lost its flower, but every place that is embellished with flowers and perfumes, it is there that he alights and lives.

Love is represented here as an infant god, which moreover conforms with a certain tradition. A few lines higher, Agathon criticized Phaedrus, the author of the first discourse, for having said (basing this upon the authority of the Orphics, of Hesiod, of Parmenides) that Love is the first and the most ancient of the gods. Agathon affirms that he is the youngest. It must be understood that the two propositions, however contradictory, are true, that Love is absolutely ancient and absolutely young.

Agathon uses the stories of war between the gods in the Hesiodic genealogies as argument; these would not have taken place, he says, if Love, who is the pacifier of the gods, had been present; 'instead there would have been friendship and peace, as at present, since Love reigns over the gods'.

195c. . . . . φιλία καὶ εἰρήνη ⟨ἦν⟩, ὥσπερ νῦν ἐξ οὗ Ἔρως τῶν θεῶν βασιλεύει.

One does not at first see the point of such an argument, since nowhere in his work does Plato indicate that he attaches importance to these Hesiodic legends. But in Aeschylus' tragedy, Prometheus puts an end to the war between Zeus and the Titans and instals Zeus upon the throne. He says also: 'Who else than I has traced for these new gods the limits of their privileges?' And Agathon says further on that it is Love who has taught each god to exercise his proper function. Notice here that in naming Love the King of the Gods, Agathon makes him the equal of Zeus; this has only the appearance of opposition to the equation with

Prometheus; which Plato seems to have been very willing to indicate.

What Plato says of the fluidity of Love, which impregnates the whole soul even while at first passing unseen, is to be brought in line with the comparisons of the Gospels between the Kingdom of Heaven and the leaven, the grain of mustard seed, the salt, etc. . . It is always a question of that capital conception which is that the supernatural in nature is at once infinitely small and infinitely active.

The relationship remarked by Plato between the beauty of the form, the proportion, and the fluidity, is extremely remarkable. It is apparently a simple allusion to a theory which he supposes known to his readers. Now that theory renders perfect account of the incomparable beauty, never equalled, of Greek sculpture before Phidias. The statues are made in such a manner that the stone seems a fluid substance which has run in layers and then set in a perfect equilibrium. The relationship between the fluidity and the equilibrium comes from the fact that a fluid cannot be made immobile except by equilibrium, unlike the solid, which is maintained by an internal coherence. The fluid is thus the perfect balance, as Archimedes was later to demonstrate. Furthermore equilibrium implies proportion, which was also to be demonstrated by Archimedes. This passage from Plato and some others seem to show that there was already at that time knowledge of the mechanical theories of which we possess, under the name of Archimedes, a rigorously geometric exposition. This is, more-over, very natural. Proportion and beauty were inseparable in the eyes of the Greeks, and it follows that what was fluid should always and everywhere be beautiful. These few lines from Plato, and their marvellous concordance with the appearance of Greek statues, show how much at that epoch art was indissolubly linked, not simply in its inspiration but in the most intimate secret of its technique, with religion and philosophy and, by their intermediary, with science. We have lost this unity, we whose religion should be the most incarnate of any. We must rediscover it.

The lines concerning Love and the flowers makes one think of the Song of Songs: 'My beloved is gone down into his garden . . . he feedeth among the lilies' (*Song of Solomon*, vi, 2 ,3).

> 196b.   The most important is that Love neither causes nor sub-
> mits to injustice, be it among the gods or among men. For, when
> suffering happens to him he does not suffer by force, for force
> cannot reach Love. And when he acts, he does not proceed by force,
> for each one consents to obey Love in everything. That agreement
> which is made by mutual consent is righteous, according to the
> laws of the 'City royal'.

These lines are perhaps the most beautiful in Plato. Here is the very centre of all Greek thought, its perfectly pure and luminous core. The recognition of might as an absolutely sovereign thing in all of nature, including the natural part of the human soul, with all the thoughts and all the feelings the soul contains, and at the same time as an absolutely detestable thing; this is the innate grandeur of Greece. Today one sees many people who honour might above all, whether they give it that name or other names possessed of a more agreeable sound. One also sees many, how-ever, in rapidly decreasing number, who despise might. This is because they are ignorant of its powerful effects. They lie to themselves, if need be, in order not to learn about it. But who knows the whole extent of the empire of might and at the same time despises it? (T. E. Lawrence, the liberator of Arabia, was one but he is dead) and perhaps some Christians very near to saintli-ness, but seemingly few. And yet this double understanding is perhaps the purest source of love for God. For to know, not abstractly but with the whole soul, that all in nature, including psychological nature, is under the dominance of a force as brutal, as pitilessly directed downward as gravity, such a knowledge glues, so to speak, the soul to prayer like a prisoner who, when he is able, remains glued to the window of his cell, or like a fly stays stuck to the bottom of a bottle by the force of its urge toward the light. There is correlation between the words of the devil in the Gospels: 'all this power will I give thee, for that is delivered unto me' and 'Our Father which art in heaven'.

This double knowledge concerning might was not common in Greece either, but it was sufficiently widespread to impregnate the whole civilization, at least during the best epoch. First of all, it is the very inspiration of the poem of the *Iliad*, and sheds light upon almost every one of its parts. The same is true for Greek tragedy, for the historians and a large part of the philosophy.

Here is another aspect of that double knowledge. Today, faced by an act of violence, some people accord their sympathy to him who exerts violence, others to him who suffers it. There is cowardice in each of these two attitudes. The best among the Greeks, beginning with the poet or poets of the *Iliad*, know that all that submits to or that exerts might is in the same way and in the same measure subject to its degrading empire. Whether one wields might or whether one is wounded by it, in whatever manner, its contact petrifies and transforms a man into a thing. That alone deserves to be called the good which escapes from its contact. But God alone escapes from this contact, and partly also those men who, by love, have transported and hidden a part of their souls in Him.

Such a conception of might alone permits one to distribute equitably the same compassion among all beings who are entirely plunged beneath its empire, and thus to imitate the equity of the heavenly Father who sheds the rain and the light of the sun equitably over all. Aeschylus has an admirable word to express this equity. He names Zeus, Ζεὺς ἑτεροῤῥεπής, Zeus who inclines to both sides (*Suppliants*, V, 403).

Plato, in this passage, affirms as strongly as possible that that alone is just which is completely withdrawn from contact with might. Now there is but one faculty of the human soul which might cannot touch, either to influence the use of it or to prevent its use. This is the faculty of consent to the good, the faculty of supernatural love. This is also the only faculty of the soul from which no brutality of any sort can proceed. It is therefore the only principle of righteousness in the human soul. The analogy obliges us to think that this is also the principle of divine justice. But since God is perfectly just, he is entirely Love.

This Love, which is God himself, acts, since he is God, but he acts only so far as he obtains consent. It is thus that he acts upon the souls of men. It is even thus that he acts upon matter, since, according to the *Timaeus* 'necessity has been vanquished by the persuasion of wisdom'.

A more surprising thing for a God, for him who is the king of all the Gods, for the supreme God, is that he not only acts, he submits: πάσχειν means at once to be modified, to submit, to suffer. From which comes πάθημα, the Greek word employed to designate the Passion. Love is modified, submits, suffers, but not by constraint. Therefore by consent.

Here once again one thinks of Prometheus. The word ἑκών, which designates consent and by which Plato expresses that perfect justice, which is the monopoly of Love, recurs several times in Aeschylus, tragedy, with insistence, or else replaced by synonyms. Prometheus had gone to take his place beside Zeus against the Titans, ἑκόνθ' ἑκόντι (v. 218); he went there willingly and there he was willingly received. Later he wilfully accomplished, with consent, the act which causes his disaster, ἑκών, ἑκὼν ἥμαρτον, (v. 266), 'voluntary, voluntary was my fault'. Despite his affliction, never shall he do the will of Zeus so long as he is in chains, but only when freed. However, the reconciliation with Zeus will come. If one holds to the literal and vulgar sense of the account, one might believe that Prometheus had to obtain his liberty by stress of blackmail, but in reality there would be friendship, willing reconciliation, consented to from both sides, εἰς ἀρθμὸν ἐμοὶ καὶ φιλότητα σπεύδων σπεύδοντί ποθ' ἥξει, 'He shall be there one day aspiring to that union and that friendship with me to which I aspire' (v. 190). (See further on for more extensive citations.)

Finally, of course, one is led by this Love, who is God, and who nevertheless suffers, but not by force, to think of the Christ.

Notice that if one couples the perfectly just being, who is a man and whom the anguish of the crucifixion puts to death, and Prometheus, who is an immortal god and whom a tradition recalled by Hesiod regarded as perpetually crucified, one reaches the analogy of the double conception of the sacrifice of Christ, sacrifice which has once been consummated, but which, by the Mass, renews itself perpetually to the end of the world.

The kinships between the perfectly righteous one, Prometheus, Dionysus, the Soul of the World, on the one side, and on the other, Love, makes apparent beneath all these names a single and same Personage, who is the only Son of God. One could add Apollo, Artemis, celestial Aphrodite and many others.

All these concordances, short of denying the historic character of the Gospels, which it would seem difficult to do sincerely, carry no threat to the faith, but are on the contrary an overwhelming confirmation of it. They are even necessary. One sees everywhere—notably the lives of the saints show it clearly—that God wanted to bind Himself with respect to us in such a manner that even His goodness, to be exercised, has need of our prayer. He can give infinitely more than we can ask, for, at the moment when one asks, one does not yet know the fullness of the good contained in what one asks. How could God have given His only son to the world if the world had not asked for Him? This dialogue makes history infinitely more beautiful. In showing this beauty one could give contemporary intelligences that shock which they need to bring a new attention to the Christian faith.

If one said to them: 'This prodigious ancient civilization, with its art which we admire from so far beneath it, with this science which it has entirely created and which is the basis of our own, with its conception of the city forming the frame of all our opinions, and all the rest, all this was produced by the thirst, prolonged during centuries, for that source which finally sprang up and toward which today you do not even turn your eyes. . . .'

If divine Love is the perfect model of justice, and that because he is withdrawn from all contact with might, neither can man be righteous except by preserving himself equally from contact with might, and he cannot preserve himself except by love. By love he must imitate Love, who never suffers anything without having consented to suffer it. It is also possible for man to be like this. It suffices for him to consent fully, at every instant, with love for the order God has created in the world, to all wounds without the least exception which the course of events may bring him. This unconditional 'Yes' which is pronounced in the most secret point of the soul, which is but silence, is entirely withdrawn from all danger of contact with force. Nothing else in the soul can be withdrawn from it. This method is simple. There is no other. This is *amor fati*, it is the virtue of obedience, the Christian virtue excellent above all others. But this 'Yes' has no virtue unless it is absolutely unconditional, then truly it transports that part of the soul which pronounces it to heaven, to the bosom of the Father. It is a wing.

To imitate divine Love, no force must ever be exercised. Being creatures of flesh and caught in necessity, we can be constrained by a strict obligation to transmit the violence of the mechanism of which we are a wheel; for example as leaders over subordinates, as soldiers over enemies. It is often very difficult, painful, and agonizing to determine just how far strict obligation goes. But it is simple to take as rule with regard to others, and even with regard to oneself, in the wielding of stress, never to go even so much as a millimetre beyond strict obligation, and that not only concerning what is properly called constraint but also in all the disguised forms of constraint; pressure, eloquence, persuasion which we use as psychological aids. Not to use any kind of constraint, either toward others or toward oneself outside the domain of strict obligation, and not to hope for any kind of power or prestige, even in view of the good, this is also a form of the virtue of obedience. Outside what is strictly obligatory, it is necessary only that what is best in a human being, the reflection of God in him, or rather the orientation of his desire toward God, should act by radiance, as an inspiration upon himself and those who approach him. This is the manner in which divine Love acts and this we should imitate.

196c. Besides justice, he has the highest degree of temperance. For all concur to define restraint as the mastery of pleasures and of desires, and to say that no pleasure is stronger than Love. If they are less strong, they are mastered by Love and he rules over them. If he is master of pleasures and of desires, Love above every being possesses temperance.

Again a few marvellously profound lines. We are only intoxicated by the pleasures which fill us, and beyond that, fill us to running over, the desires which thrust us toward them. Then there is drunkenness, then satiety and disgust, almost hate, then once again desire. But Love is the essential desire, infinite, absolute, which no joy can fill to the point of running over. Even in God, the infinite joy which infinitely fills, and the infinitely insatiable desire for Love, exist together. As for us, we have infinity in us only in this central desire. Our joys can be but finite and the desire for Love in us consumes and burns them as they arise in us. We can only be intemperate by mistake, when we believe that to satisfy ourselves we only need joys that are a little greater than those we have known till now. If one gives himself up to love, if for the sake of love one accepts to have always within one a never fulfilled yearning, one has the perfection of restraint.

For the rest, the word restraint, like temperance, is very inadequate to translate σωφροσύνη, a much stronger and more beautiful term. It is this term which is constantly employed in the *Hippolytus* of Euripides to designate perfect and virginal chastity. Purity would perhaps be better.

196d. And as for valour, Ares himself is no match for love. For it is not Ares who holds Love, it is the love of Aphrodite which holds Ares captive, as the story goes. He who holds is stronger than he who is held. He who masters, he who is the most valorous of all must be absolutely courageous.

This seems to be a jest, but that is an appearance. It is clear that Ares cannot conquer Love, since force cannot attain to Love. Love conquers Ares. Which is to say that warlike bravery (and all the analogous forms of bravery also) has need of a love to inspire it. A base love inspires a base courage, an absolutely pure love inspires an absolutely pure valour. But without love there is only cowardice. Love never exerts force, carries no arms, and yet is the source from which those who carry the sword draw their virtue. Love contains in itself the eminent form of that virtue; contains in itself all there is of valour which is other than brutality and armed might. One does not know how to imitate valour so long as one does not possess more warlike valour than the warriors, and that without being a warrior.

196d.   What is left concerns wisdom . . . this God is so learned in poetry that he even makes poets of others, for whoever is touched by Love becomes a poet though formerly he had no part in the Muses. Herein we find proof that Love is a good artist, and in a word for all artistic production which has a relationship with music. For none can give or teach another what he lacks, or what he does not know himself. And in the generation of living beings none will deny that Love possesses the wisdom which begets and develops all creatures. And do we not know that in the practice of the arts and techniques all that this God has taught us to do is admirable and brilliant, while all that he does not touch is gloomy? Apollo invented archery, medicine, prophecy, being guided by love and desire, thus he is also the pupil of Love. So too the Muses invented music, Hephaestus metallurgy, Athena weaving, Zeus the government of gods and of men. It is thus that the affairs of the gods were ordered when Love was born, the love of beauty, of course, for Love has nothing to do with ugliness. Formerly, as I have said, many atrocities were committed among the gods because they were under the dominance of necessity. When this God appeared, the desire for the beautiful caused every good to surge up among the gods and among men. Therefore it appears to me that Love himself is first absolutely beautiful and perfect, and that he is the cause of all others becoming so.

By this enumeration of the four virtues one sees that in Plato's mind, justice, temperance, courage and wisdom are not natural virtues. Supernatural Love is their inspiration and immediate source, and they cannot proceed from elsewhere. The intelligence, where it is creative, in true poetry, and even in techniques where it discovers things that are truly new, proceeds directly from supernatural love. Herein is a capital truth. It is not the natural capacity, the congenital gift, nor is it the effort, the will, the work, which in the intelligence has sway over the energy capable of making it fully efficacious. It is uniquely the desire, that is, the desire for the beauty. This desire, given a certain degree of intensity and of purity, is the same thing as genius. At all levels it is the same thing as attention. If this were understood, the conception of teaching would be quite other than it is. First one would realize that the intelligence functions only in joy. Intelligence is perhaps even the only one of our faculties to which joy is indispensable. The absence of joy asphyxiates it.

The lines wherein Love is represented as the instructor of all the techniques without exception brings out even more clearly than all before love's resemblance to Prometheus, who says in Aeschylus: 'all the techniques have come to mortals from Prometheus'. He says also that Zeus himself is subjected to Necessity, which condemns him to a misfortune from which he, Prometheus, alone can free him. This is again an analogy.

The role of Love as the author and developer of all that lives, brings him near to Dionysus and Artemis, as well as to Osiris. There is an interweaving of symbols here. As among plants and animals, the union of the sexes is the image of supernatural Love, so the increase of the semen and sperm produced by this union from at first infinitesimal particles is the image of the development of the Kingdom of God in us. It is the meaning of Persephone's pomegranate seed, the mustard seed, and the grain of wheat in the Gospels. The property of chlorophyll to draw energy from the sun is also an image of the mediatory function of divine Love.

197d.   It is he who empties us of hostility, who fills us with friendship, thus establishing every sort of reunion by which we can join with one another, who makes himself our guide at feasts, in choruses and sacrifices. He brings us courtesy and sends away rudeness. He gives kindness liberally; he never gives hate. He is favourable to the good, an object of contemplation for the wise, of admiration for the gods. He is worthy to be followed when one has no share in him, to be treasured when one belongs to him. He is father of tender delights, of delicacies, of graces, of allurement, of desire. He attends to all that is good, he neglects what is bad. In trouble, in fear, in desire, in reasoning, he is the pilot, the warrior, the guardian, the perfect saviour, he is the leader of all the gods and of all men, the beautiful and perfect guide whom every man should follow with the singing of beautiful hymns, joining in with his beautiful voice by which his song touches the spirits of all the gods and of all men.

THE DISCOURSE OF SOCRATES

In this work Socrates does not speak in his own name, he repeats the teachings given him by a very wise woman who came to Athens to make a sacrifice and who, by this sacrifice, rid Athens of the plague for ten years. Her sex, the circumstances and the words pertaining to initiation and mystery which she ceaselessly employs, show sufficiently that he is talking of a priestess of the Eleusinian religion. The *Symposium* is a sufficient reply to those who believe that Socrates and Plato despised the mysteries. In it also there is a sufficiently clear indication that the doctrine contained in this work does not issue from philosophical reflection but from a religious tradition. Diotima begins by making Socrates understand that Love, being the desire for good, for beauty and for wisdom, is neither good nor beautiful, nor wise, although, of course, it is not ugly, nor evil nor ignorant either. Agathon said a while back that Love possesses the plenitude of goodness, therefore of beauty and of wisdom. Here also it must be understood that contradictory propositions are at the same time true. And since Love suffers nothing except by his own consent, he has voluntarily emptied himself of good, of beauty and of wisdom.

Diotima explains that Love is a δαίμων. The use of the word δαίμων in Greek is very variable. Sometimes this word is synonymous with θεός, God. Sometimes it indicates a being who is above man, who belongs to a supernatural world, but who is beneath the divinity, something similar to an angel. Furthermore, οἱ θεοί, the gods, sometimes also means something resembling the angels. And again δαίμων sometimes means demon in the sense in which we use that word. But here Diotima defines the use which she makes of the word δαίμων. It designates the mediators, the intermediaries between man and God.

> 202e.   Love is an intermediary between that which is mortal and that which is immortal . . . it is a great 'daimon'. And all of this species is intermediary between God and man.
>
> 'And what is his function?' I asked. To interpret and to transmit human messages to the Gods, and divine messages to men, from one side the supplications and sacrifices, from the other commandments and answers to those sacrifices. The function of this species, being in between these two, is to fill and span this breach between them, thus reuniting all to itself. By him the art of prophecy and that of the priests, of sacrifices, of mysteries and of incantations, are accomplished. God does not mingle himself with man, it is uniquely by means of Love, or, the daimon that there is intercourse and dialogue between the gods and men.

It is difficult to know whether in Plato's mind there are several mediators of this species or a single one. He says that there are several of them and that Love is one of them, but does he really mean several beings, or several aspects of the same being? In the lines above he uses the singular as if there were but a single being.

The word ἑρμηνεῦον, he who interprets, compares Love and Hermes, the interpreter, the messenger of the Gods, who accompanies souls into the other world, the inventor of the lyre, the god who was an infant prodigy.

In these lines Love appears as the ideal priest.

It must not be forgotten that this god who is priest and mediator, who is between the divinity and man, is the same who is, according to Agathon's speech, at least equal to Zeus, who teaches Zeus the art of government, who is the king of the gods.

Plato affirms here, as categorically as possible, that apart from divine mediation there can be no relationship between God and man: 'No man cometh unto the Father except by me.'

Concerning the arithmetical and geometric idea of mediation, and the role of this idea in the first discovery of science, see further on.

MYTH OF THE BIRTH OF LOVE

203b.   When Aphrodite was born, the Gods held a banquet, and among them was the son of Wisdom, Resource. After the meal, as is the custom at banquets, Want came to beg. She stood by the gates. Resource, drunk with nectar, for wine did not yet exist, entered the Garden of Zeus, and being heavy, he slept. Want, because of the lack of resource in her, sought how to have a child by Resource. She stretched out beside him and became pregnant with Love. This is why Love is born the companion and attendant of Aphrodite, having been engendered at the feast of her birthday. Moreover, he is by nature in love with the beautiful, and Aphrodite is beautiful. As the son of Resource and of Want, the fortune of love is to be as follows: first he is perpetually in want, and he is far from being delicate and beautiful as the multitude believes him. He is hardened and dried up, barefoot, without a roof, always stretched out upon the ground, sleeping in front of doorsteps, along the road-sides, in the open air. Having his mother's nature, he is always the companion of privation. But like his father, he is enterprising in regard to beautiful and good things, he is courageous, always busy, always intense, a formidable hunter, perpetually weaving some sort of plan, desirous of wisdom, creating his own resources, philosophiz-ing the whole length of life, accomplished in lamentations, and incantations and in remedies, a skilful sophist. His nature is neither immortal nor yet mortal, but sometimes the same day he flourishes, and lives while he is resourceful, or sometimes then he dies and again is resuscitated by reason of his father's nature. . . .

204b. Wisdom is of supreme beauty and Love is love of the beautiful, therefore necessarily he loves Wisdom. and loving Wisdom, Love is the intermediary between the knowing and the ignorant. The cause of this is in his birth. For his father is wise and resourceful, his mother wants wisdom and wants resource.

Each word of this delicious myth deserves to be meditated. Five (six?)[1] personages are named in it: Aphrodite, Wisdom, Resource, Zeus, Want and Love. However unsatisfying, one cannot translate πόρος except by Resource. For πόρος has but two meanings, one is: way, passage, path; the other is: means, resource. To make an opposition to Want, the meaning resource must be taken. But the other meaning, that of a way, must also be retained. The Chinese call God Tao, which is to say *Way*. Christ said: 'I am the Way'. But on the other hand πόρος is the origin of the verbs πόρω and πορίζω, literally to open the way, but above all to procure, to supply, to give. If one could take πόρος in its secondary sense, that would be to say gift. . . . In Catholic theology Gift is the proper name of the Holy Spirit. In the *Prometheus* of Aeschylus there is a play of words upon this verbal root, which is repeated three times in a few lines.

τὴν πεπρωμένην χρὴ αἶσαν φέρειν, 'I must endure the fate which has been given me' (perfect past participle of πόρω). θνητοῖς γέρα ·όρων, 'having given a privilege to mortals'. πυρὸς πηγὴν . . . ἡ ιδάσκαλος . . . πέφηνε καὶ μέγας πόρος, 'the source of fire . . . which appeared as an instructress and a great resource (or a great treasure, or a great gift) (lines 103, 108, 111). In this last verse the name of πόρος is applied to fire. It is very probable besides that here is a play of words between πῦρ and πόρος. In the Heraclitan trinity, which appears so clearly in the hymn to Zeus by Cleanthes, Zeus, the Word, the lightning or the fire, the fire corresponds to the Holy Spirit, which is also the case for several New Testament

[1] The text reads *five* personages, but six are listed. (Tr.)

passages (Matthew iii, 11: 'He shall baptize you with the Holy Ghost, and with fire'; Luke xii, 49: 'I am come to send fire on the earth', etc.) and Pentecost. First one may conclude that the being whom Plato names Poros is the Holy Ghost, since there is a close connection known to Plato and perhaps also to Aeschylus, between this myth and that of Prometheus.

Poros is the son of Metis, Wisdom, whose name is almost the same as that of Prometheus. Hesiod relates that the Earth, Gaia— which in Aeschylus is identical with Themis and the Mother of Prometheus—one day warns Zeus that Wisdom was destined to have a son stronger than he who would dethrone him. . . . To avoid this danger, Zeus eats Wisdom. She was his wife and already pregnant. The child issued from the head of Zeus, this was Athena.

Here the child is Poros. If Wisdom is the Verb, there is nothing astonishing in this genealogy: *Qui ex Patre Filioque procedit.*

Notice in passing that Athena is the Goddess of the olive tree and that the oil in the Catholic religion is associated with the sacraments which have a relationship most particularly with the Holy Spirit. Notice also that Athena is called Tritogene, epithet whose most natural meaning is 'the third born'. In Egypt, it is in the Temple of Athena, according to Herodotus, that the sepulchre of Him who has suffered a Passion, is found. Athena is the only divinity besides Zeus who handles the Aegis (shield), an object closely connected with lightning, which is the symbol of the Holy Spirit. But here it is not a question of Athena.

Celestial Aphrodite is divine beauty. The beautiful being the image of the good and the good being God. She is, also, the Word. Herodotus says that she passed into Persian religion under the name of Mithras. Mithras is probably that Wisdom which seems to have appeared in the sacred books of Israel after the exile. Love was conceived on Aphrodite's birthday, he is her loving companion. These are two aspects of the same divine person, who is here Aphrodite as the image of God, and Love as the mediator.

This Love, represented a while ago as the king of the gods, is here a miserable vagabond. This is as he wanted it. He wanted to be born the son of Want. If what is meant here is the Incarnation, and if Poros is the Holy Spirit, the concordance is perfect.

There cannot be a want more radical than that of being other than God. This is the poverty of every creature. Creation in its distress invented the plot of a poor woman who hopes to associate herself in some enduring manner with the destiny of a rich man, without his knowledge, by bearing him a child even in spite of himself. She imagined having a child by God. She chose a moment when God was drunk and sleeping. There must be intoxication and sleep for such madness.

(Plato says that wine had not been discovered at that time. Doubtless he wanted thereby to stress the identity of Love and of Dionysus.)

The child is destitute, as is appropriate for our brother. This delicious picture of poor and vagabond Love, always lying upon the bare ground, inevitably reminds us of St. Francis. But before St. Francis, of the Christ who is poor and homeless, having no place to lay his head. He also had poverty for companion.

In this picture there are also words which seem intended to recall the Prometheus of Aeschylus. Love's body is withered, αὐχμηρὸς. So is Prometheus' body, προσαυαινόμενον, and the bloom of his complexion faded (23). Love sleeps, ὑπαίθριος, in the open air, without shelter. Prometheus is also ὑπαίθριος (113) and αἰθέριον κίνυγμα, suspended in the air (157). 'Sophist' is Hermes' insult to Prometheus. The word μηχανή—procedure, trickery, deceit, contrivance, means, invention—also recurs endlessly in this tragedy. (One finds it also in the *Electra* of Sophocles immediately after Electra's recognition of Orestes.) Aeschylus speaks of Prometheus' talent for finding remedies, φάρμακα.

Love is said to be a formidable hunter, which makes him akin to Artemis, but akin also to another who gathered sinners about him. And Prometheus also captured in the hunt θηρῶμαι (109), the source of fire.

Love appears here as the author of the most complete harmony, in the Pythagorean sense, that is to say of the unity between the contraries which themselves are the most contrary possible, known as God and Want.

> 205d.   To sum up, all desire is desire for the good and for happiness. . . . There is a doctrine which says that those who seek the other half of themselves are the ones who love. My theory affirms that love has for object neither the half nor the whole, unless such happens to be the good. For men will consent to have their feet and their hands cut off if these seem evil to them. I do not think that anyone cherishes what belongs to him, unless he calls that the good which is his own, and belongs to him, and unless he names evil that which is not his own. There is no other object of love for men than the good. . . . Briefly, it is by means of love that one perpetually desires to possess the good.

Here is a refutation of Aristophanes' myth, the myth of the man cut in two, whose halves search for each other. But here again it must be understood that the affirmations which contradict one another are both true. The phrase which seems to contradict Aristophanes' myth, as often happens, only reveals its true significance. We are indeed incomplete beings who have been cleft by violence, fragments perpetually starving for their complementary part. But contrary to what Aristophanes' myth would seem at first sight to indicate, this complement cannot be in our own likeness. Our completion is the good; that is, God. We are fragments torn from God.

'There is no other object of love for men save the good.' Consequently, none but God. We need not search how to put the love of God in us. It is the very foundation of our being. If we love anything else, we do so by error as the result of mistaken identity. We are like someone who runs joyfully down the street toward a stranger whom at a distance he mistook for a friend. But whatever is mediocre in us, by an instinct of self-preservation and by means of all sorts of lies, tries to hinder our recognition of the truth: what we perpetually love, from the first to the last instant of life, is nothing else than the true God. Because as soon as we recognize this, all the mediocrity in us is condemned to death.

In the *Republic* there is another passage dealing with this theme which is still more beautiful and more powerful.

X

THE 'REPUBLIC'[1]

VI, 505e. [The good is] what every soul seeks, the motive of all its actions, whose importance is sensed, but the soul, being at a loss, is unable completely to grasp its essence. Thus concerning the good the soul cannot have a firm belief as it has about everything else. This is the reason why the soul lacks other things also, and the usefulness which they may have.

Plato compares this love of the good, which is always in us, to the power of sight, and the revelation of good he compares to the light. From this concept the following metaphorical description of conversion stems:

VII, 518b. The instruction [of the soul] is not what some declare it to be. For they affirm that knowledge, not being in the soul, they will put it there, as if one might put sight into blind eyes. Whereas the theory which I will expound teaches that the faculty of understanding, and the organ of this faculty, is innate in the soul of each one. But it is as if one were unable to turn one's eye towards the light, away from darkness, without turning the whole body. Likewise it is with the whole soul that one must turn oneself from what is becoming (the temporal) until the soul becomes strong enough to endure the contemplation of reality, and all that is most luminous in that reality; which we have already declared to be the good.

---

[1] From *Les Intuitions Préchrétiennes*, pages 71-86.

The art of conversion consists in this, that it is the easiest and most rapid method of bringing someone to turn round. This is quite a different thing from a method for putting sight into the soul, which we know it has already. But that sight is not well directed, and it does not look where it should. It is this that the soul must find a means to learn.

Here again is that word μηχανή, which recurs so often in Plato and in the tragedies where the theme is one of salvation and of redemption.

This saying from the *Symposium*: 'my theory is that love has for object neither the half, nor the whole, of man's self . . . there is nothing that men love except the good', is of great depth. It destroys the false idea of egoism. Men are not egoists. They are not able to be. Their misfortune is in not being capable of it. God is the only egoist. Man can only approach a certain shadow of love for himself when he knows how to see himself as God's creature, loved by God, redeemed by God. Otherwise a man cannot love himself.

What is generally named egoism is not love of self, it is a defect of perspective. People give the name of disaster to that alteration of a certain arrangement of things which they see from the point where they are; from that point, things at a little distance are invisible. The massacre of one hundred thousand Chinese hardly alters the order of the world as they perceive it, but if instead a fellow worker has a slight rise in pay which they have not, the order of the world is turned upside down! This is not love of self, it is that men, being finite creatures, only apply the idea of legitimate order to the immediate neighbourhood of their hearts.

They have the power of choice and of transposing the heart where their treasure is. It is not so uncommon to see a man absolutely devoted to another man, known or unknown to him personally, to a wife, to a child, to a party, to a nation, to whatever collectivity, to no matter which cause. One cannot in that case say he is an egoist. But the mechanism of the faulty perspective remains the same, and the errors remain no less grave. Such devotion is not higher, or is hardly higher, than what is called egoism.

To escape from the errors of a false perspective the only way is to choose one's treasure and to carry one's heart beyond space, and beyond the world, to God.

The principal image which Plato uses in the *Republic*, notably in the passage about the cave, the image of the sun and of sight, shows exactly what love is in man. One would make a complete mistake in believing that the metaphor of the cave relates to knowledge and that sight signifies the intelligence. The sun is the good. Sight is then the faculty which is in relationship with the good. Plato, in the *Symposium*, says as definitely as possible that this faculty is love. By the eyes, by sight, Plato means love. This image makes the impossibility of egoism evident, for the eyes cannot see themselves. The unreality of things, which Plato so powerfully depicts in the metaphor of the cave, has no connection with the things as such; the things in themselves have the fullness of reality in that they exist. It is a question of things as the object for love. In this reference they are like shadows cast by puppets.

To understand this one must recall the image of the great beast. Human society, and any collectivity contained within that society, is likened to the great and powerful beast whose tastes and aversions are to be studied and assembled into a treatise by the man who has charge of caring for him. Morality is nothing else. For those who teach it 'call whatever pleases this animal good, and whatever displeases him evil, and they have no other criterion. They call righteous and beautiful those things which are necessary, being incapable of seeing, or of showing others, to what degree the essence of the necessary differs from that of the good.' (vi, 493c.)[1]

There is no other morality than that taught by the great beast and his keepers, unless God Himself descends to reveal the true good to the soul.

[1] Cf. p. 86.

492e.   There is not, there has not been, there never will be any
other moral education than theirs, I mean to say, my friend, no
other human education. God, according to the proverb, must be
excepted. For this must be well understood, he who is saved and
becomes what he ought to be according to his nature, so long as
states are constituted as they are, to speak exactly, one should say
that he has been saved by a predestination from God.

Except for the predestined who have come out of the cave, or
are on the right road for coming out of it, we all choose for
treasure those values that have their substance in social prestige.
This is true even for the desires which seem only to have reference
to individuals. So is the desire of the lover. 'Love without vanity
is only an invalid,' said La Rochefoucauld. The pleasures of
eating and drinking are much more social than they seem at
first. Riches, power, advancement, decorations, honours of every
kind, reputation, recognition, are values of an exclusively social
order. Under the names of beauty and of truth almost all artists
and scholars seek social prestige. The etiquette of charity, of love
for one's neighbour, is generally a cover for the same article.

Social prestige, as the name itself indicates, is pure illusion, is
a thing which has no existence. And yet power is ninety per cent.
prestige, and power determines all in this world. That is the lesson
in Grimm's story of the *Valiant Little Tailor*, and in numberless
other similar stories. A little man, having crushed seven flies at a
single stroke, goes about the world proclaiming: 'I have killed
seven at one stroke.' A country that is on the point of being
invaded by a very powerful enemy takes him for its general. As
he has never been on horseback, the day before the battle he has
himself tied to a horse for practice. To his great dismay the horse
sets off at a gallop and carries him straight into the enemy camp.
The enemy, seeing the sudden arrival of a galloping horseman,
believe him to be followed by a vast army, and they flee in
disorder. The little tailor becomes son-in-law to the king.

This story expresses the pure truth. There is nothing more real
in this world than war, including also under that name the con-

flicts of masked power, for it is this, as Heraclitus says, that makes slaves of some and freemen of others, men of some, gods of others —but false gods, of course. This is the active principle of social life, whose fortune, success or failure, is almost entirely determined by this illusion. War is made up of prestige. It is this which permits the devil to say to Christ: 'all this power and the glory of them is delivered to me'. The supreme social value, or rather the unique value, is prestige. That is indeed a shadow. That is a lie.

The things which project this shadow are, according to Plato, puppets. Which means real but artificial things, fabricated like imitations of real and natural things. These puppets are the social institutions. The good which the miser believes he can find in gold is an illusion, a shadow. On the contrary, money, as a means of exchange, is a good, but a purely conventional good. There is a great difference between illusion and convention. Conventions have a certain reality, but of a secondary and artificial order. If gold were no longer used as money, there would be no more value in gold. If no other value than its usefulness in the circulation of merchandise were found in it, there would be nothing but good in gold, a limited and low-ranking good, but pure, without admixture of evil. The good contained in the smile of Louis XIV, that good for which the greater part of all Frenchmen of the seventeenth century would have suffered death, was a shadow. The good belonging to the person of a man upon a throne was real, but only by relation to the institution of royalty and in a purely conventional manner. Like the institution of currency and the institution of royalty, such are the puppets whose shadows pass across the wall of the cave. In all human institutions the images of truths of a supernatural order are to be found, and this is why Plato calls them puppets, likenesses of real beings. But one only recognizes this resemblance in so far as one considers them as institutions when one has turned from the shadows, that is to say, from the prestige. To do this is supposed to be easy, is even thought of as already accomplished. For the prestige about which one really cares is not recognized as such. The total renunciation of all prestige is what St. John of the Cross calls spiritual nakedness. By that alone one attains to God. This is why Christ said: 'The Father who is in secret.' Which is the same as the Father who is in heaven. Unfortunately for us, the secret is equally distant, at a distance as inaccessible as the heavens. For all of us, save a few of the elect, are consumed by desire for prestige.

Christ, throughout his life, had very little prestige. He was totally stripped of it after the Last Supper. Even his disciples completely abandoned him. Peter denied him; Peter who today is wrapped in a mantle of prestige deriving from the Church and twenty centuries of Christian history. During the life of Christ it was extremely difficult to continue wholly faithful to him in his misfortune. Today there is an even greater difficulty. Because of his prestige, which acts as a screen, it is possible to be faithful even to death without being sure that it is to him one is faithful. Doubtless it is not impossible even to be a martyr without ever leaving the cave, without ever having turned one's gaze from the shadows which follow one another across the wall.

Plato knew that the real and perfect justice must be without prestige. It is the absence of prestige, and not the physical suffering, which is the very essence of the Passion. The words of Isaiah: 'a man of sorrows and acquainted with grief' have their true meaning only for a people among whom illness is despised. But the physical suffering would have been too little. A suffering of penal character was required, for man is not truly stripped of all participation in social prestige until penal justice has cut him off from society. No other type of suffering has this character of irreducible, ineradicable degradation which is essential to the suffering inflicted by penal justice. But it must truly be penal justice; that which strikes common criminals by common justice. A man who is persecuted and condemned for his fidelity to a cause, to a collectivity, to an idea, or a faith, for national, political or religious reasons, does not undergo this total loss of prestige. Even though he should submit to death after many and atrocious tortures and humiliations, his sufferings would be very far from those of the Cross. For all that the Christ may have been in a certain sense the first of the martyrs, their master and the model for them all, in another sense it is still more true to say that he was not a martyr at all. He was ridiculed like those madmen who take themselves for kings; then he perished like a common criminal. There is a prestige belonging to the martyr of which he was entirely deprived. Also he did not go to his martyrdom in joy, but in a swoon of all the powers of the soul, after having vainly implored his Father to spare him and having vainly asked men to console him.

This essentially and irreducibly penal character of redemptive suffering is what the Greeks understood very well. It is manifest in the story of Prometheus. It is also in the picture of the sufferings of the perfectly just man, as Plato depicts it in the *Republic*.

II, 360e. Let us subtract nothing either from the injustices of the unjust man, nor from the justice of the just man, but consider each one in his own way. . . .

361b. Take the just man, let us show him forth by our words. Simple and generous, desiring, as Aeschylus says, not the appearance but the reality of the good. Let us take away all appearance. . . . Let him be shown naked of all things except justice, . . . that while committing no injustice he may have the greatest reputation for injustice in order that this may be a touchstone for his justice, to prove whether this evil reputation, and the consequences thereof, make him waver, or whether on the contrary he continues steadfast, seeming all his life to be unjust but being truly just. In this way, when they shall have gone [i.e. the just and the unjust man] each one to the last degree either of justice or of injustice, it will be discernible which of the two is the happier. . . .

361e. Being in that state of soul, the just man shall be whipped, given over to torture, to chains, his eyes shall be burnt out and, at last, having been inflicted with all possible sufferings, he shall be hanged. Then he will know that he should desire not the reality, but the appearance of justice. . . .

367b.   Show us by your words not only that justice is better than injustice. Show us by what process each by itself makes him who possesses the one or the other, either good or evil. Take away the appearances. For unless you take from its true appearance, replacing it by the false appearance, we shall say you praise not justice itself but the reputation of justice, that you blame not injustice but the reputation of injustice, and that, without letting it be seen, you are really advising us to be unjust. . . .

367e.   Therefore show us by your words not only that justice is better than injustice but by what process each, itself, and by itself, makes him who possesses it good or bad, whether manifest or hidden before the Gods and before men.

Who this perfectly just man might be, in case he should exist, is seen in another passage from the *Republic*.

V, 472b.   If we find what justice is, should we hold that the just man must in no way differ from that, but must be in all regards absolutely just? Or should we be satisfied if he comes nearer than all others and has within him a greater share of justice?

Let us be satisfied with that approximation, said he.

But to arrive at an ideal, we were trying to discover what justice is in itself, and what the ideal of a perfectly just man is, in case he might exist, and what he would be if he did exist, and the same for injustice and the unjust; so that we might contemplate each one and to see if happiness or its contrary is manifest in one or the other. For we are obliged to admit that for ourselves likewise, whoever most resembles one or the other model, must also live a life which most resembles the life of that model. But it has not been our goal to show that all this *does* exist, any more than a painter who might paint his ideal of the most beautiful man, and might be satisfied with his picture, should be considered an inferior painter because he could not prove that such an ideal man exists in reality.

Compare this text with the following from the *Theaetetus*:

176a.   One must strive to flee from this world as quickly as possible. This flight is an assimilation in God . . . this assimilation consists in becoming righteous and holy with wisdom. . . .

176b. God is never in any manner unjust, he has the supreme degree of justice, nothing resembles him as much as that man among us who is perfectly just. . . .

176e. In reality, my friend, there exist two ideals, the one divine and perfectly blessed, the other deprived of God and entirely wretched. But these people do not see that this is so, and in their extreme and stupid madness they are not aware that by their unjust actions they resemble the second, and are unlike the first.

Upon the subject of the pity due these madmen and the rarity of truly just men, there are a few lines in the *Republic*.

II, 366c. Whoever has a sufficiently certain understanding that justice is the greatest good, will be full of forgiveness for unjust men, he will not be angry with them, knowing that except for those in whom a supernatural aversion for injustice is innate, and those who shun it after having learned about it from others, none is just by his own means. It is cowardice, or old age, or some other weakness which makes them blame the injustice which they are incapable of accomplishing.

There is in these lines something resembling an echo of the words: 'Forgive them for they know not what they do.' The lines concerning likeness with the evil model recall the words: 'I come not to judge . . . they judge themselves.'

The passage concerning the perfectly just man demonstrates the idea of divine incarnation more clearly than any other Greek text. For it is stated in the *Phaedrus* that justice in itself is to be found in that place beyond the skies where Zeus, accompanied by the gods and the souls of the blessed, takes his repast. It is evident in the *Timaeus*, that what is found in this place is the Soul of the World, the only Son. Just (or righteous) men are simply very close to justice itself, they have a very large share in it. But in order that a man 'in no way differs from justice itself', should be the same in all respects as justice, 'divine Justice, from beyond the skies, must descend upon earth', μηδὲν . . . αὐτῆς ἐκείνης διαφέρειν, ἀλλὰ πανταχῇ τοιοῦτον εἶναι οἷον δικαιοσύνη ἐστίν.

Plato understandably refused to demonstrate that such a thing could be possible. Yet one cannot doubt his intimate thought on the subject if one remembers that the centre of his inspiration is the ontological proof, the certainty that the perfect is more real than the imperfect.

The ideal model for relatively just men can only be a perfectly just man. Relatively just men exist. If their model is to be real, he must have an earthly existence at a certain point in space, and at a certain moment of time. There is no other reality for a man. If the ideal cannot have this existence, it is nothing but an abstraction. Is it acceptable that an abstraction should constitute the model and the perfection of real beings?

One must be careful to notice how Plato clearly affirms that justice in itself is not a sufficient model. The model of justice for men is a just man.

It is he, doubtless, who is also the divine and blessed ideal spoken of in the *Theaetetus*. When Plato speaks of assimilation with this model, the word assimilation is used in the sense which we give it today, it is a question of resemblance. Only the meaning is more rigorous, it is of a resemblance such as exists between two geographical maps of two different scales, wherein the distances are different but the relationships are identical. For the word assimilation in Greek, and especially for such a Pythagorean as Plato, is a geometrical term which refers to the identity of relationships, to proportion. When Plato speaks of assimilation in God, it is no longer a question of resemblance, for no resemblance is possible, but one of proportion. No proportion is possible between men and God except by mediation. The divine model, the perfectly just man, is the mediator between just men and God. On this topic, see below a discussion of the Pythagorean doctrine.

Everything leads us to believe that the absolutely just Love of the *Symposium* is the same as the divine model of the *Theaetetus* and the perfectly just man of the *Republic*.

In order that divine justice may be a model for men to imitate, it is not enough that it should be incarnate in a man. In that man, moreover, the authenticity of perfect justice must be manifest.

For that, the justice in him must be seen without prestige, naked without honour, divested of all the brilliance which the reputation of justice gives. This is a contradictory condition. If justice is apparent, it is veiled in appearance, enveloped in prestige. If it does not appear, if no one knows that the perfectly just man is just, how can he serve as model?

The true justice is as much disguised by the appearance of justice as by the appearance of injustice. In order that it may serve as model it must therefore be seen naked, without appearance; it must appear without disguises. This is absurd. In that case justice could serve no purpose by coming down on earth. Its presence is useless if our contact with it is missing.

We have access only to appearances, and these appearances are of the prestige belonging to the kingdom of might. The appearance of justice is a means of procuring certain advantages for oneself, and one obtains it by certain processes. It belongs to the mechanisms of necessity. There is an infinite distance between the nature of the necessary and that of the good. Our world is the kingdom of necessity. The appearance of justice is of this world. Real justice is not of this world.

Insoluble contradictions have a supernatural solution. The solution of this one is the Passion. But it is truly a solution only for those souls who are entirely possessed by the light of grace. For the others, the contradiction endures. During the days when Christ was, as Plato would have him, completely stripped of all appearance of justice, even his friends themselves were no longer wholly conscious of his being perfectly righteous. Otherwise could they have slept while he suffered, could they have fled, have denied him? After the Resurrection the infamous character of his ordeal was effaced by glory, and today, across twenty centuries of adoration, the degradation which is the very essence of the Passion is hardly felt by us. We think now only of the suffering, and of that but vaguely, for the sufferings which we imagine are always lacking in gravity. We no longer imagine the dying Christ as a common criminal. St. Paul himself wrote: 'If Jesus Christ be not risen, then is our faith vain.' And yet the death on the Cross is something more divine than the Resurrection, it is the point where Christ's divinity is concentrated. Today the glorious Christ veils from us the Christ who was made a malediction; and thus we are in danger of adoring in his name the appearance, and not the reality, of justice.

In short, only the penitent thief has seen justice as Plato conceived it, naked and perfect, veiled beneath the appearance of a criminal.

Plato, in going so far as to suppose that the perfectly just man is not recognized as just, even by the gods, had premonition of the most piercing words of the Gospel: 'My God, my God, why hast thou forsaken me?'

The reason which Plato gives for the suffering of the perfectly just man is different from redemption, different from the substitution of punishment which appears in Christianity, and even earlier, in the *Prometheus* of Aeschylus. But there is a bond between the two ideas. It is because of the regression set working in human affairs by original sin that there is this incompatibility between the appearance and the reality, and it is this which obliges perfect justice to appear here below in the form of a condemned criminal. If we were innocent, the appearance would be of the same colour as the real and have no veil to be torn away.

It is because the appearance is false that the desire, which constitutes our very being, even though it may be desire for the good, inclines us only toward evil, so long as our conversion is not accomplished.

The image of the cave illustrates the workings of conversion in a manner that is well known.

In the *Symposium* one also finds depicted the stages by which the soul comes to salvation. Here it is a question of salvation by beauty.

Diotima begins with the theory of carnal Love as being the desire to beget in beauty with a view to immortality. The instinct for reproduction is what is most indestructible in animal life. The desire of eternity in us goes first by mistake toward that material image of eternity. By a mysterious alliance, of which Plato does not attempt to give an account here, the desire for propagation is aroused only by beauty, carnal beauty, since the subject here is carnal procreation. Correspondingly, among those who are capable of it, spiritual beauty excites a desire for spiritual generation; thus love causes virtues, understandings, and works of the spirit, to be born.

(Notice that here in the matter of carnal love Plato does not regard as legitimate any but that directed to the generation of children. This refutes the slanderous accusations of immorality.)

The stages of the soul's progress described here lead from the consideration of physical beauty in a person, to the consideration of physical beauty wherever it is found. From there they lead to the beauty of souls, from there to the beauty in laws and institutions, from there to the beauty in the sciences, till finally one reaches the consummation of love, the contemplation of beauty in itself.

Symposium

210c. That he may see the beauty of the sciences and look at last toward the fullness of beauty. On

211a. ... turning to the vast sea of the beautiful to contemplate it, he shall beget vast doctrines, full of many beautiful and great thoughts in a generous philosophy, until, being thus fortified and ripened, he discerns a unique science which is this one of beauty.

210e. For he who has come to this point in amorous education, by considering beautiful things in their correct order, arriving at the accomplishment of love suddenly shall contemplate a miraculous sort of beauty. ... This is first of all eternally real, neither begotten, nor mortal, which neither waxes nor wanes. Moreover this is not a beauty which is beautiful from one side but ugly from another, beautiful at one time but not at another, beautiful in one reference, and ugly in another, beautiful for some, ugly for others. And this beauty will not appear to him as a face, or as hands or anything corporeal; not as a theory, nor any science, nor will it appear as dwelling in any thing, or in any living being upon earth or in heaven or anywhere. But this will be beauty itself, by itself, with itself, of a unique nature, eternally real. All beautiful things have part of this beauty, but in such a way that when they are born or perish, beauty itself suffers no increase, no decrease nor the least modification.

211b.   He who undertakes the contemplation of this beauty has very nearly attained to perfection.

211c.   . . . he knows at last what beauty is.

212a.   Do you believe that the life of a man who searches into such a matter, who uses the appropriate organ to contemplate and to unite himself with it, can be mediocre? Consider this; what we have here is the only being who sees the beautiful with that faculty capable of seeing it. To him it will be given to beget, not sham virtues, for he has not laid hold upon a phantom, but real virtues, because he has laid hold on the real. And in creating and nourishing true virtue, it is accorded him to be the friend of God; and if ever a, man became immortal that man will become so.

212b.   In this work it would be difficult for human nature to find a better collaborator than Love.

These passages show how mistaken are people who consider Plato's ideas as solidified abstractions. Here it is a question of a spiritual marriage with the beautiful, by the grace of which the soul truly begets virtues. Further, the beautiful does not reside in anything. It is not an attribute. It is a subject. It is God.

The formula which recurs so often in Plato, αὐτὸ καθ' αὐτὸ μεθ' αὐτοῦ, itself, by itself, with itself, might well have a relationship with the Trinity. For this formula indicates two relationships within a unity. And is it not exactly thus that St. Thomas defines the Trinity?

Moreover, Plato says that he who contemplates beauty itself has almost reached the goal. Which indicates that there is still something else. In the myth of the cave, the object of contemplation, immediately before the sun, is the moon. The moon is the reflection, the image of the sun. The sun being the good, it is natural to suppose that the moon is the beautiful. In saying that he who has attained to beauty has almost arrived, Plato suggests that the supreme beauty is the Son of God.

In Greek mythology, absolute beauty is the heavenly Aphrodite. (Be it said in passing that it is all the more appropriate to use the moon as symbol of the Son because the moon undergoes a diminution, a disappearance, then a rebirth; thus it is also an appropriate symbol of the Passion.) Certain details of the myth of Osiris are thereby explained. A bull represents Osiris because of its horns in the shape of a crescent moon. Its body is divided in fourteen parts, and fourteen is the number of days which separate the full moon from the new moon. Isis assembles thirteen of these, and thirteen is the number of lunar months in the year. As for Isis, she is identical with Demeter, the mother goddess whose symbol is the earth. Plutarch also says that Osiris is the principle of the humidity that fecundates, of the sap, the role which the ancients attributed to the moon. Zagreus, elsewhere, is called by Nonnus the horned new-born one who rises to the throne of Zeus and seizes the lightning. The Titans catch him in a trap. The Titans are twelve in number, and in comparing their names in Hesiod with the signs of the Zodiac, one finds several correspondences. To escape from the Titans, Zagreus takes many forms, the last one is that of a bull, that is to say once again a horned form. In this form the Titans kill him. This story may easily be applied to the phases of the moon. Sophocles calls Dionysus: 'Fire, leader of the chorus, of the breathing stars, guardian of nocturnal voices, overseer.' All that applies very well to the moon, the last epithet, on account of the months. Notice, with a bit of forcing, one can find again in the day, the month, and the year, something like the relationship of a mean. The *Hippolytus* of Euripides is explicable only by the identification of Artemis and Dionysus, for Hippolytus is an Orphic initiated in the mysteries of Eleusis. The bow of Artemis and of Apollo, the lyre of Apollo and of Hermes (for Hermes according to the Homeric hymn is the child-god inventor of the lyre) are by their shape reminiscent of the crescent moon. Pan also is a horned god. His name means 'all'. Plato consistently calls the Soul of the World 'the all', and he says, in the *Cratylus*, that Pan is the λόγος. Many things in mythology are clarified if one admits the assumption that all that relates to the moon, to horns (because they are images of the moon) and to vegetable sap symbolizes the Word. Furthermore, such divinities as Athena and perhaps Hephaestus seem to correspond to the Holy Spirit. Athena was begotten by Zeus alone. Hephaestus is the son of a legitimate union. All the other children of Zeus come of adulterous unions. Here is perhaps a symbol of scandal, of the madness which the union of God with his creature implies. In this case, all these children of Zeus would be names of the Word. Hestia the central fire is the Holy Spirit.

Absolute beauty is something as concrete as sensible objects, something which one sees, but sees by supernatural sight. After a long spiritual preparation one has access to it by a sort of revelation, of rending: 'suddenly he shall perceive a species of miraculous beauty'. This is the description of mystical experience. This beauty is not modified when beautiful things are born and perish; although they are beautiful they are so only by participation in Absolute Beauty. Here is the supreme consolation for all evil. No evil does harm to God. He who sees absolute beauty by the only organ to which it is visible, which is to say supernatural love, places his treasure and his heart beyond the reach of all evil.

The order of the stages enumerated by Plato may surprise us. From sensible beauty he passes to the beauty of souls, that is, to moral beauty, the splendour of virtue. When we want to praise an action which has truly touched us, we don't say 'that is good' but 'that is beautiful', and if the Saints attract us, that is because we sense the beauty in them. Virtue only touches us in so far as it is beautiful. The analogy between this beauty and the beauty of the senses is very mysterious. A certain equilibrium, almost impossible to define, is the secret of one and of the other. Laws and institutions constitute another equilibrium which is placed as if at the intersection of virtue and of natural necessity. But it is almost impossible to make out exactly what Plato has in mind: whether it is the city as a metaphor, as an enlarged image of the soul, as it is studied in the *Republic*, or a study of the harmony belonging to social relations, such as one finds in the *Statesman*. Anyway, the Pythagorean idea of harmony as the union of contraries, and the combination of that which limits and of that which is limitless, must successively dominate these three studies. As for beauty in the sciences, this is nothing but the beauty of the order of the world perceived through the most rigorous necessity, that which is the material of mathematical demonstration, for Plato calls both pure and applied mathematics sciences. It is not surprising that this should be the last stage. To him who lovingly contemplates the order of the world, there shall come a certain day and moment when suddenly he shall contemplate another thing, a miraculous sort of beauty.

Along the way which Plato here traces there is no question of God so long as real contact has not been established by mystical experience, and not even then except by allusion. This is the very opposite of the Christian way, in which one speaks of God long before having the least suspicion of what that word signifies. The advantage is that this word by itself has a power, the disadvantage is that the authenticity is lessened. In any case, the difference should not lead to a misunderstanding of the essential identity.

In all the preceding texts, Plato speaks of God in His relation with creation or with Man. But there is one text wherein he describes the perfect and infinite joy in God Himself. This is in the *Phaedrus*.

246e. The great sovereign, Zeus, driving his winged chariot, advances the first, watching over the order of all things. He is followed by an army of gods and demi-gods arranged in eleven bands. For Hestia alone remains in the dwelling of the gods. . . . Whoever wishes to, and is able, follows them, for envy has no place in the choir of the gods. When they go to a repast, or a banquet, they advance to the extreme limit of the sky, and there they mount higher. . . .

247b. The souls of those called the immortals, when they arrive at the summit, go outside, and standing there upon the outer side of heaven, they allow themselves to be carried by its rotation, gazing upon all that is outside the vault of heaven. Of what lies beyond heaven, no poet of this world ever has sung, nor ever shall sing, worthily. This is how it is. . . . Essence without colour, without form, without anything that can be touched, yet real, which can only be contemplated by the master of the soul, by the mind. In this place dwells that essence with which true knowledge is concerned. Just as God's thought nourishes itself upon spirit and upon understanding without mixture, so that of every soul receiving what is appropriate for it throughout time, gazing upon pure being, loves and contemplates and feeds upon truth and is happy, until the revolution of the universe has brought it back to its original place. During the course of the rotation, the soul sees justice itself, it sees purity, it sees knowledge, not that knowledge which is concerned with birth, which is different in different things, nor that which today we call by that name, but the science which is real in the reality of its being, and so all the realities, these the soul contemplates and nourishes itself upon them. Then, slipping back into the interior of heaven, the soul returns home.

God's life consists in an act of God upon God which is at once contemplation and communion. God eternally feeds upon Himself and contemplates Himself. Those are two relationships in God. This is the Trinity.

The great misfortune of man, very keenly felt in childhood, which explains many human deviations, is that for him gazing and eating are two different operations.

249e. Every soul, by its nature, has contemplated reality. . . . The remembrance of the things of the other side of heaven is not easy for every man on this side. . . . Only a few are sufficiently endowed with memory. These, when they see an image of things there, are seized with giddiness, lose possession of themselves, but because they lack sufficient discernment, they are ignorant of what is happening to them. Justice, purity and all the virtues of the soul, are without the least splendour in their earthly copies, but a few people with difficulty and by dim instruments, approaching the reflections of them, contemplate the essence of their models. But formerly beauty itself was resplendent to see. . . .

250d.   Beauty shone with them in their procession. And here below we seize beauty itself in its manifest splendour through the clearest of our senses. For sight is the sharpest of the bodily senses; but it does not see wisdom. For wisdom would create terrible loves, if like beauty it produced a manifest image of itself which was capable of being seen. And the same is true for all that we love. In fact, only beauty has this destiny: to be what is the most manifest and the most loved.

Plato says that here below we see beauty itself. In his vocabulary that means the Idea of the Beautiful itself, the divine Beauty itself, is accessible to human senses. But a few lines further on, speaking of the trouble caused by the beauty of a human being, he says that this beauty is called by the same name as the Beautiful in itself. It is therefore not the Beautiful in itself. God's own beauty made manifest to the senses, is the beauty of the world, as it is set forth in the *Timaeus*. The beauty of a young girl, or of an adolescent youth, is only of the same name.

The beauty of the world is God's own Beauty, as the beauty of the body of a human being is the beauty which belongs to that being.

But wisdom, righteousness and the rest cannot appear to us in the world but only in a human being who will be God.

XI

THE PYTHAGOREAN DOCTRINE[1]

PYTHAGOREAN THOUGHT is for us the great mystery of Greek civilization. It recurs everywhere, again and again. It impregnates almost all the poetry, almost all the philosophy—and especially Plato, whom Aristotle regarded as a pure Pythagorean. The music, the architecture, the sculpture, all the sciences of ancient Greece proceeded from it; so did arithmetic, geometry, astronomy, mechanics and biology—that science which is fundamentally the same as ours today. Plato's political thought (in its most authentic form, which means as it is formulated in the dialogue the *Statesman*) also derives from the Pythagorean doctrine. It embraced almost all secular life. There was then, between the different parts of secular life, and between the secular life as a whole and the supernatural world, as much unity as today there is separation.

The roots of Pythagorean thought extend far into the past. In expounding the concept which is at the centre of that doctrine, Plato evokes a very ancient revelation, which is perhaps the primal one (*Philebus*). Herodotus says that the Pythagoreans borrowed a large part at least of their beliefs from Egypt. Another ancient historian, Diodorus Siculus, I believe, points to the analogies between Pythagorean thought and Druidic thought, which, according to Diogenes Laertius, was considered by certain

[1] From *Les Intuitions Préchrétiennes*, pages 108-171.

people as one of the sources of Greek philosophy. This, be it said in passing, obliges one to regard the Druidic religion as of Iberian origin, just as the metaphysical and religious part of Greek civilization comes from the Pelasgians.

(In parenthesis, Iberians, Pelasgians—that is to say, Aegean-Cretans—Trojans and those assimilated with them, Phoenicians, Sumerians, Egyptians, seem before historic times to have formed around the Mediterranean a homogeneous civilization impregnated by a supernatural and pure spirituality. Most of these peoples are named in the Bible among the descendants of Ham. The Hellenes, according to the testimony of Greek writers, arrived in Greece ignorant of all spirituality; one may perhaps draw from that a valuable conclusion for the mass of Indo-Europeans. The Bible shows that there was very little spirituality in Israel until the Exile. Among the Indo-European peoples, whom one generally associates with Japhet, and those whom the Bible regards as Semites, there are two kinds. Certain of these learned from the peoples they conquered and thus assimilated the spirituality of their captives. Such were the Celts, the Greeks, the Babylonians. Others remained obstinately deaf. Such were the Romans, probably the Assyrians and the Hebrews, at least until the Exile. If, with these thoughts in mind one re-reads the episode of Noah's three sons, it appears that Noah, who was a pure being, righteous and perfect, had a mystic intoxication accompanied by nakedness in the mystical sense. It appears that Noah had a revelation in which Ham shared and in which his two other sons refused to share. The curse which fell upon the descendants of Ham would then be what is, in this world, the lot of those who are too pure. The Hebrews would have arranged the story in a way to justify the massacre of the Canaanites. But Ezekiel expressly compares Egypt to the tree of life of the earthly Paradise, and Phoenicia, at least at the beginning of his story, to the cherub standing by the tree. If this view of the matter is correct, a current of perfectly pure spirituality would have flowed across Antiquity from pre-historic Egypt to Christianity. This current flowed through

Pythagorism. (Notice that there is indeed a revelation connected with Noah, for the Bible says that God formed a covenant with humanity in the person of Noah, a covenant whose sign is the rainbow. There can be no covenant between God and man without revelation. Deucalion, the Greek Noah, is the son of Prometheus, to whom Aeschylus and Plato attribute a revelation.)

Today the depth of Pythagorean thought cannot be perceived except by using a sort of intuition. And one cannot exercise such an intuition except from inside; that is to say, only if one has truly drawn spiritual life from the texts studied.

The fundamental texts are two or three fragments from Philolaus, a passage from the *Gorgias*, two from *Philebus* and one from *Epinomis*. There are also some formulas, or equations, transmitted by Aristotle or Diogenes Laertius. To all that, a formula of Anaximander should be joined, although it is not Pythagorean. And one should, as far as possible, bear in mind the totality of Greek civilization.

Here are the texts:

Philolaus[1]

2 [B 47].   All realities are necessarily either limiting or unlimited, or else limiting and unlimited. Unlimited alone they cannot be, since it is manifest that realities proceed not only from what limits, nor only from what is unlimited. Clearly the order of the world and of things contained therein has been brought into harmony, starting from that which limits and from that which is unlimited.

3 [B 49].   From the beginning there would not even be anything susceptible of being known, if all were unlimited.

4 [B 58].   All that is known involves number. For without number nothing can be thought or known.

8 [B 150].   Unity is the principle of everything.

7 [B 91].   The first to be arranged, the one at the centre of the sphere, is named Hestia.

[1] Diels.

11 [B 139-160]. The essence of number and of harmony are totally untouched by the false, for that does not belong to them. Falsehood and envy belong to the nature of what is unlimited, un-thinkable and without proportion.

The false never projects its spirit into number, for number is essentially hostile to the false. The truth belongs to the same family as number, truth is of the same root.

The essence of number is productive of understanding, a guide and a master for whoever is in perplexity or ignorance about any-thing. For there would be no clarity in things, either in themselves or in their mutual relations, if there were not number and its essence. Therefore number, fitting all things into the soul through sense perception, renders them comprehensible and mutually in accord, and gives them a body and separates by force each relationship of unlimited and limiting things.

6 [B 62]. The following concerns nature and harmony. What is the eternal essence of things, and nature in itself, can be known only by the divinity and not by man, or else man may know only this. Not even one of the realities could be known to us if there were not the basic essence of things, of which the order of the world is com-posed, some limiting, the others un-limited. Since the principles which uphold all are not alike, nor of the same root, it would be impossible that the order of the world should be based upon them if harmony were not brought in by some means. For things that are alike and of the same root have no need of harmony; those that are not alike, nor of the same root, nor of the same station, need to be locked together under key by a harmony capable of maintaining them in the world order.

10 [B 61]. Harmony is the unification of what was mixture. It is the common thought of what is separately thought. Cf. Pro-clus' (Euclid's commentary).

Plato teaches us many marvellous concepts concerning the divinity by means of mathematical ideas. And Pythagorean wisdom also makes use of mathematical ideas as a cloak to hide the mystical way of the divine doctrine. This is the case for all the

The Pythagorean Doctrine

'*Hieros Logos*' and Philolaus in his *Bacchantes* and the whole teaching method of Pythagoras concerning the divinity.

Plato, *Gorgias*, 507d

Everyone should flee from licentiousness as fast as his feet can carry him . . . and not give liberty to desires or try to satisfy them, a termless evil, a robber's existence! For whoever concedes to his desires cannot be in close friendship either with another man or with God; for he is not capable of communion; and for whoever there is no communion, there is no friendship. And according to the sages, Callicles, it is communion which unites the heavens and the earth, the gods and men, in friendship, order, restraint, justice. Because of that, this universe has been named order (cosmos) and not disorder and licentiousness. But it seems to me that you do not give your attention to these things, although you are instructed. You have not observed how great a power geometrical equality is both among the gods and among men. You believe you should strive to acquire. This is because you do not pay attention to geometry.

Philebus

16b.   No more beautiful way either does, or ever can, exist. I am perpetually in love with it, but often it escapes me and leaves me abandoned, not knowing what to do. . . . Herein is a gift of the gods to men, that at least is clear to me. And from whatever habitation of the gods it was tossed by a Prometheus, there came at the same time an illuminating fire; and the ancients who were better than we are, and lived nearer the gods, have transmitted this tradition to us. Here it is: that the realities called eternal derive from the one and the many, and carry, implanted within them, the determinate and the indeterminate. We should therefore, since this is the eternal order of things, seek to implant a unity in every kind of domain. We shall find it, for it is there. Once we have grasped this unity, we should examine duality, if that is present, or else trinity, or some other number. Then the same subdivisions must be made upon each one of the subordinate unities. Finally, what at the beginning appeared not only as one, and many, and unlimited at once, appears also with a definite number. One should not apply the idea of the indeterminate to the plurality until one has perfectly well seen the number of that plurality, that number which is the intermediary between the indeterminate and unity. Only then one should abandon the specific unity of all things and lose oneself in the indeterminate [infinite]. The gods then, as I was saying, have transmitted this method of research for our use in learning, and in teaching. The educated men of our time fix unity at random, and the plurality more quickly or more slowly than should be, and pass from the unity to things which are indeterminate; the intermediary escapes them.

26b. It is from this that the seasons and all that is beautiful are produced for us, from things which are indeterminate, and from that which includes limit, from the fact that there is admixture or exchange between them.

(Limit is 'the essence of the equal and of the double and of all that prevents contrary things from diverging among themselves, but brings them into proportion and accord by imprinting number [measure] upon them'.)

31d. I say therefore that when harmony in living beings is dissolved among us, nature itself is at the same time undone and suffering appears. When harmony is restored with a return to the primitive state, joy appears, if in a few words, as briefly as possible, such great matters may be spoken of.

Epinomis, 990d

He who has learned this science (arithmetic) should then pass immediately to what is called by the ridiculous name of geometry. This is the assimilation of numbers which do not by nature resemble one another, an assimilation made manifest when referred to the properties of plane figures. That this marvel is not human but divine is clear to anyone who can think. Next the numbers that are cubed, corresponding to the properties of solids, and those which were not alike are made so by another art which, when it was discovered, was named stereometry. What is supernatural and miraculous for those who can contemplate and think is that, while power perpetually revolves around duplication, all of nature is marked by the form and the essence of the relationship of opposites, according to each proportion. First that of the numerical double, the relation of one to two, which is double. Then the proportion in respect of power, and that which is again double, going even to what is the solid and palpable, extending from one to eight. And in the relationship between one to two there are the means, the arithmetical mean, at equal distance from the least and the greatest, the harmonic mean, which exceeds the least and is surpassed by the greatest according to the same ratio—thus eight and nine between six and twelve. . . . between these two means, situated at equal distance from both, is found the ratio of which I speak, by which men have received a share in the knowledge of the agreement of voices and of proportion in the apprenticeship of rhythm and of harmony. This is a gift from the blessed choir of the Muses.

Timaeus, 31c

It is impossible that the disposition or arrangement of two of anything, so long as there are only two, should be beautiful without a third. There must be come between them, in the middle, a bond which brings them into union. The most beautiful of bonds is that which brings perfect unity to itself and the parts linked. It is geometrical proportion which, by essence, is the most beautiful for such achievement. For when of three numbers, or of three masses, or of any other quantity, the intermediary is to the last as the first is to the last, and reciprocally, the last to the intermediary, as the intermediary to the first, then the intermediary becomes first and last. Further, the last and the first become both intermediaries; thus it is necessary that all achieve identity; and, being identified mutually, they shall be one.

The Gospel according to St. John

xvii, 11, 21, 22, 23.   Holy Father, keep through thine own name those whom thou hast given me, that they may be one, as we are . . . That they all may be one; as thou, Father, art in me, and I in thee, that they also may be one in us. . . . And the glory which thou gavest me I have given them; that they may be one, even as we are one: I in them, and thou in me, that they may be made perfect in one.

xvii, 18. As thou has sent me into the world, even so have I also sent them into the world.

x, 14, 15. I am the good shepherd, and know my sheep, and am known of mine. As the Father knoweth me, even so know I the Father.

xv, 9, 10. As the Father hath loved me, so have I loved you: continue ye in my love. If ye keep my commandments, ye shall abide in my love; even as I have kept my Father's commandments, and abide in his love.

Symposium

202d. Love . . . is a great 'daimon', and that which is 'daimon' is intermediary between God and man . . . being in the middle of the one and the other, it fills the distance in such a manner that the whole is bound together in itself.

210d. That he may see the beauty of the sciences . . . turning toward the vast sea of the beautiful.

Fragment of Anaximander of Miletus

Such is the point of departure of the birth of things and the term of their destruction which occur in conformity to necessity; for they suffer a chastisement and an expiation from each other because of their injustice, according to the order of the times.

The ancient historians of philosophy have transmitted Pythagorean formulae to us, some of them clear and marvellous, as this one which perhaps concerns carnal death, but which surely concerns detachment: μηδ' ἀποδημοῦντα ἐπιστρέφεσθαι, 'that he who leaves his country does not return.' (Cf. Luke ix, 62: 'No man, having put his hand to the plough, and looking back, is fit for the kingdom of God.') And again: 'Let the man who enters a temple adore, and not speak, nor be occupied with anything temporal.' 'He who follows the divinity is before all things master of his tongue.' (Cf. Epistle of St. James: 'look not at Thyself in a mirror beside a lamp.') This perhaps means not to think of oneself when one thinks of God; 'lack not faith for any marvel concerning the gods and divine dogma'; 'not to gnaw his heart'; 'what is most just is the sacrifice, what is most wise is number'. This has a strange ring: 'Break not the bread, for it is of no advantage in the judgment of the other world.'

Certain formulae are very obscure, as this one which Aristotle cites with disdain: ἡ δικαιοσύνη ἀριθμὸς ἰσάκις ἴσος, 'justice is a number to the second power'. Or one cited by Diogenes Laertius: φιλίαν ἐναρμόνιον ἰσότητα, 'friendship is an equality made of harmony'.

The key to these two equations, and many others cited above, is the idea of a mean proportional and of mediation in the theological sense, the first being the image of the second.

It is known that among the Pythagoreans one is the symbol of God. Several testimonies, among them Aristotle's, affirm this of Plato. Heraclitus also, who is very near to the Pythagoreans in many respects—contrary to common opinion—said: 'The One, that unique sage, wishes, and wishes not, to be named Zeus.'

The Pythagoreans considered all created things as having each a number as its symbol. It is of little importance here how they conceived this number and the link between that number and the thing.

Among these numbers, some have a particular bond with unity. These are the numbers which are of the second power or square. By a mediation there is between them and unity an equality of relations $\frac{1}{3} = \frac{3}{9}$.

When the son of God is in a reasonable creature, as the Father is in the Son, that creature is perfectly just. Plato says in the *Theaetetus* that justice is assimilation in God. Similarity, in the geometrical sense, means proportion. The mysterious equation of the Pythagoreans, and that of Plato which seems clear, have the same meaning. Whoever is just becomes to the Son of God as the Son is to His Father. Doubtless this identity of relations is not literally possible. However, the perfection proposed to man should be something like that, for in many of St. John's precepts the same words are repeated to designate the relationship of the disciples to Christ and of the Christ to His Father. The allusion to a mathematical equation of proportion is evident.

The passage in the *Timaeus* on proportion might strictly be interpreted as uniquely applicable to mathematics if there were not several sharp indications to the contrary meaning. First, in the passage itself. 'The most beautiful of bonds is that which, to the highest degree, renders itself one with the terms which are bound.' This condition is truly realized when not only the first term but also the bond itself is one; that is to say, is God. This interpretation, it is true, is not self-evident. But Plato uses the same linking word in the *Symposium* to define the mediatory function of Love between the divinity and man. Then Proclus' words are clear: 'Plato teaches us many marvellous doctrines concerning the divinity by means of mathematical ideas.'

Clearer still is this phrase from Philolaus (to be joined with that cited above): ἴδοις δέ κα οὐ μόνον ἐν τοῖς δαιμονίοις καὶ θείοις πράγμασι τὰν τῶ ἀριθμῶ φύσιν καὶ τὰν δύναμιν ἰσχύουσαν, ἀλλὰ καὶ ἐν τοῖς ἀνθρωπικοῖς ἔργοις καὶ λόγοις παντᾶ καὶ κατὰ τας δημιουργίας τὰς τεχνικὰς πάσας καὶ κατὰ τὰν μουσικάν.

'One can see what powerful effect nature and the virtue of number has not only in religious and divine things but everywhere in human acts and reasonings both in the working of various techniques and in music.'

(Religious and divine things, δαιμονίοις καὶ θείοις πράγμασι, that is to say, if one refers back to the *Symposium*, all that concerns God as such and as Mediator.)

This is clear. It is as if Philolaus said one would be wrong to believe that our mathematics applies only to Theology. It applies also, by extension, by the effect of a wondrous coincidence, to human matters, to music, and to the techniques.

If the passage from the *Timaeus* on proportion has, besides its obvious sense, a theological sense, this meaning can be none other than that of Christ's words cited by St. John, which are so very similar.

The allusion is evident. Just as the Christ recognized Himself as Isaiah's man of sorrows, and the Messiah of all the prophets of Israel, He recognized Himself also as being that mean proportional of which the Greeks had for centuries been thinking so intensely.

If one considers whole numbers, one sees they are of two sorts; those that are linked to unity by a mean proportional, such as 4, 9, 16 on one hand, and on the other hand all the others. If the first are an image of perfect justice, as the Pythagoreans say, we resemble the others, we who are in sin.

Was it by force of so intense a search for a mediation of these wretched numbers that the Greeks discovered geometry? Such an origin for geometry would agree well with Philolaus' saying cited above, and also with that in the *Epinomis*, a work which one feels to be wholly impregnated by Plato's oral instruction: 'What one ridiculously calls geometry is the assimilation of numbers not naturally similar among themselves. Their assimilation becomes manifest when applied to the properties of plane figures, and this, to whoever is capable of thought, is a marvel which comes from God and not from men.'

These lines define geometry as the science of what is today called real numbers, of which the square root of two or of any other number not square is an example. They exactly define geometry as the science of irrational square roots.

The notion of similar triangles, attributed to Thales, relates to proportion, but not to mediation.[1] It implies a proportion of four terms: $\frac{a}{b} = \frac{c}{d}$. For want of documents one can neither accept nor reject the possibility that Thales, in studying it, intended to

---

[1] Simone Weil uses the French word *médiation* in two senses, to mean simultaneously both our word 'mediation' and also the arithmetical terms 'the mean' and 'median'. It is impossible to convey this ambiguity in English, so I have used 'mediation' throughout, even where 'mean' or 'median' would be more appropriate, as this seems to convey her thought better. —Tr.

facilitate the study of mediation (that is to say the proportion of three terms: $\frac{a}{b} = \frac{b}{c}$).

It is equally certain that if, knowing only the conditions of the similarity of the triangles, one posits the problem: To find the mean proportional between two segments, the strictly coordinated steps of thought may lead us to alter the formulation of the problem into this: To construct a right-angled triangle, given the hypotenuse and the position of the foot of the perpendicular.

The inscription of a right-angled triangle in a circle, which gives the solution of this second problem, is the theorem for which it is said that Pythagorus offered a sacrifice.

In any case, whether or not geometry had since its first origin been a search for mediation, it offered this marvel of a mediation for the numbers which were naturally deprived of it. It is said that this marvel was for a long time one of the great Pythagorean secrets. Or more exactly, their secret was the incommensurability of the terms of such a proportion. It was wrongly believed that they kept this marvel a secret because it disproved their system; they would never have been guilty of such meanness.

Among the Pythagoreans the words ἀριθμός and λόγος were synonyms. They called the irrational relationships λόγοι ἄλογοι. To bind those numbers which are not square to unity requires a mediation which comes from outside, from a domain foreign to number which can only fulfil this function at the price of a contradiction. This mediation between unity and number is in appearance something inferior to number, something indeterminate. A *logos alogos* is a scandal, an absurdity, a thing contrary to nature.

The Greeks experienced a further amazement, as the *Epinomis* testifies, to find in experienced nature this mediation as a mark, as a seal, of the supreme verity. For example in music. The scale does not contain the geometric mean as a note, but is symmetrically disposed around that mean; there is the same geometric mean between one note and its octave and between the fourth and the fifth. One sees this immediately with the numbers 6, 8, 9, 12, for $\sqrt{6 \times 12} = \sqrt{8 \times 9}$. The fourth and the fifth are themselves two kinds of mean between the notes of the octave (for $\dfrac{8-6}{6} = \dfrac{12-8}{12}$, and $12-9 = 9-6$). Such is, according to the *Epinomis*, the principle of musical harmony. In the *Symposium* it is said that harmony is an identity of ratios, *homologia*, a term which, in the most rigorous sense, must designate proportion.

All Greek science in all its branches is only the research into proportions, whether of three or four terms. It is thus that the Greeks invented the notion of function, which is simply the idea of two quantities which vary proportionately without ceasing to be linked by a fixed relationship. The first and most brilliant application of this idea to the study of nature is Archimedes' theory of floating bodies, a purely geometrical theory. What we, in our scientific conception of the world, call a law is nothing but the application to nature of the idea of function.

The soul of our science is demonstration. The experimental method differs from the grossest empiricism only by the role which deduction plays therein. According to documents actually in our possession, it seems that the Greeks were the first to have carried demonstration outside the domain of whole number by the invention of geometry and its application to the study of nature.

It is marvellous, it is inexpressibly intoxicating, to think that it is love, and the desire of the Christ, which caused the invention of demonstration to spring up in Greece. As long as the relations of lines and of surfaces were studied only with a view to a technical application, they had no need to be certain, they could be approximate.

The Greeks had such a need of certainty of divine verities that even in the simple image of these verities they had to have the maximum of certainty. Perhaps from the beginning of time men have regarded whole numbers as appropriate to serve as images of the divine truths because of their perfect precision, because of the certainty, and at the same time the mystery, contained in their relationships. But this evidence of the relationships between whole numbers is still close to sensibility.

The Greeks, by the study of non-numerical proportions, found evidence of a much higher level, quite as exact as those in which all the terms are whole numbers. Thus they found an even more appropriate image for divine verities.

That their attachment to geometry was of a religious nature is obvious not only from the few texts which bear witness to it but still more from the mysterious fact that, until Diophantus, a writer who lived during the period of decadence, they had no algebra. About two thousand years before the Christian era the Babylonians had an algebra with equations with numerical co-efficients of the second and even third and fourth degrees. It can hardly be doubted that the Greeks knew this algebra. They wanted none of it. Their algebraic knowledge, which was very advanced, is all contained in their geometry.

On the other hand, it was not the results which were important to them, not the quantity or the importance of the discovered theorems, but only the rigour of the demonstrations. Those in whom this attitude of mind was wanting were despised.

The notion of real number, arrived at by the mediation between any number and unity, was matter for just as severe demonstration, as clear as anything in their arithmetic, and at the same time incomprehensible to the imagination. This notion forces the mind to deal in exact terms with those relationships which it is incapable of representing to itself. Here is an admirable introduction to the mysteries of faith.

By this one can conceive an order of certainty, starting from uncertain and easily grasped thoughts about the sensible world, proceeding to thoughts of God which are absolutely certain and absolutely inapprehensible.

Mathematics is doubly a mediation between these two kinds of thought. It has the intermediate degree of certitude, the intermediate degree of inconceivability. It includes the précis of the necessity which governs sensible things and the images of divine truths. Finally, it has for its core the very idea of mediation.

It is easily understood that when they perceived this poetry, the Greeks were intoxicated by it; they had the right to see in it a revelation.

Today we can no longer conceive this because we have lost the idea that absolute certainty belongs only to divine things. We want certainty for material things. For the things which concern God, we are satisfied with belief. It is true that simple belief succeeds very well in having the power of certitude when it is at white heat from the fire of collective feelings, yet it remains belief for all that. Its force is illusory.

Our intelligence has become so crude that we no longer conceive that there could be an authentic, rigorous certainty concerning the incomprehensible mysteries. Upon this point there would be an infinitely precious use for mathematics, which is irreplacable in this respect.

The requirement of perfect rigour which obtained in Greek geometers has disappeared with them, and now, only within the last fifty years, are mathematicians returning to it. Today that rigour exists among them as no more than an ideal, analogous to that of art for art's sake among the Parnassian poets. But it is one of the gaps through which real Christianity may once again filter into the modern world. The requirement of rigour is not something material. When that requirement is absolute, its use in mathematics is too obviously disproportionate to its object. Its object is the relationships of quantity, and its conditions are an axiomatic reduction of all theorems to a few arbitrarily chosen axioms. In mathematics this exigence destroys itself. It must one day appear there as an exigence exerting itself in the void. On that day it will be close to being fulfilled. The need of certainty will then encounter its true object.

God's mercy preserves mathematics from being drowned in mere technique. For, wherever the science of mathematics is cultivated on the technical plane only, there is no success, even on that technical plane. This experiment has been made in Russia. The technical applications are related through pure science to a number of things which are attained only by extension, and which one never finds by seeking for them directly. This providential arrangement insures, at the heart of our basely material civilization, a core of theoretic science which is rigorous and pure. This core is one of the openings through which the breath and the light of God may penetrate. Another opening is the search for beauty in art. A third is affliction. It must enter by these openings, not by the filled places.

The formula: 'Friendship is an equality made of harmony', φιλίαν εἶναι ἐναρμόνιον ἰσότητα, is full of marvellous meanings with regard to God, with regard to the communion of God and man, and with regard to men, provided that the Pythagorean sense of the word harmony is taken into account. Harmony is proportion. It is also the unity of contraries.

To apply this formula to God it must be juxtaposed with a definition of harmony which at first sight is very strange: δίχα φρονεόντων συμφρόνησις, 'the common thought of separate thinkers'. Of the separate thinkers who think together there is, in all rigour, only one example, that is the Trinity.

Aristotle's definition, 'Thought is the thought of thought', does not comprehend the Trinity because the noun can be equally well taken in an active or a passive sense. Philolaus' formula comprehends it because the verb is active.

Contemplation of this formula leads to the best method of enlightening the intelligence about the dogma of the Trinity.

If we think of God only as one, we think of Him either as a thing, and then He is not act, or as a subject, and then to be in action He needs an object, else creation would be necessity and not love. God would not be exclusively love and good.

We, human beings, because we are subjects only by perpetual contact with an object, cannot conceive God as perfect except by conceiving Him as being at once subject and object.

But God is essentially subject, thinking and not thought. His name is 'I am'. That is His name as subject, it is also His name as object, it is also His name as contact with the subject and the object.

All human thought implies three terms, a subject which thinks, and which is a person, an object thought, and the thought itself, which is the contact between the two. Aristotle's formula 'Thought is the thought of thought', designates these three terms on condition that one takes the word thought each time in a different sense.

To represent God to ourselves as a thinking thought, and not as a thing, we have to represent these three terms in divine thought; but divine dignity exacts that these three be each one a Person, although there be a single God. Divine dignity prevents the word thought, when it refers to God, from ever being taken in the passive voice; the verb to think, when God is subject, can only be taken in the active voice. What God thinks is still a Being who thinks. This is why we say this is the Son or the Image, or the Wisdom of God.

Such is the perfect thought in so far as we men can grasp its inconceivable character. Every other representation which we can make is easier to imagine but is infinitely short of perfection. This is why the intelligence can adhere fully, and without the least uncertainty, to the dogma of the Trinity even though unable to understand it.

If friendship is interpreted as an equality made of harmony, using for the definition of harmony the common thought of separate thinkers, then the Trinity itself is the friendship above all in excellence. The equality is the equality between one and many, between one and two. The contraries, of which harmony constitutes the unity, are unity and plurality, which are the first pair of contraries. This is why Philolaus speaks on the one hand of 'the one' as first origin, and on the other hand of unity as the first created being. This he named Hestia, the central hearth, the central fire; and fire always corresponds to the Holy Spirit. The equation 'Friendship is an equality made of harmony' further includes the two relationships indicated by St. Augustine in the Trinity, equality and connection. The Trinity is the supreme harmony and the supreme friendship.

Harmony is the union of contraries. The first pair of contraries is one and two, unity and plurality, which constitute the Trinity (Plato doubtless had also the Trinity in mind as the first harmony when in the *Timaeus* he named the terms of the first pair of contraries the Same and the Other). The second pair of contraries is the opposition between the creator and the creature. In Pythagorean language, this opposition expresses itself as correlation between that which limits and that which is limitless, in other words, that which receives its limitation from outside. The principle of all limitation is God. Creation is matter brought into order by God, and this ordering action of God consists in imposing limits. Indeed this is also the conception of Genesis. These limits are either quantities or something analogous to quantity. Thus, one can say that limit is number, taking the word in its widest sense. From this Plato's formula: 'Number is the intermediary between the one and the limitless'. The supreme One is God, and it is He who limits.

In the *Philebus* Plato indicates the first two pairs of contraries in their order and marks the hierarchy which separates them when he writes: 'The reality called eternal proceeds from the one and the many and has limit and limitlessness rooted in itself.' The limit and the unlimited, that is creation whose root is in God. The one and the many is the Trinity, the first origin. Number appears in the Trinity as the second term of the opposition, and if it is identified with limit, it appears in the principle of creation as the first term. It is then indeed something like a mean proportional. It should not be forgotten that in Greek *arithmos* and *logos* are two exactly synonymous terms. The conception which Plato expounds at the beginning of the *Philebus*, a conception of marvellous depth and fertility is that all study and all technique, for example the study of language, of the alphabet, of music, and so on, should reproduce, each one at its own level, the order of this primordial hierarchy. This is unity, number in the largest and most unlimited sense. Thus the intelligence is an image of faith.

Since there is in God as creator a second pair of contraries, there is in Him also a harmony and a friendship which are not defined alone by the dogma of the Trinity. There must also be in God unity between the creative and ordering principle of limitation and the inert matter which is indetermination. For that, not only the principle of limitation but also the inert matter and the union between the two, must be divine Persons, since there cannot be any relationship in God whose terms are not Persons, just as the bond which links them must be a Person. But inert matter does not think, it cannot be a person.

The insoluble difficulties are resolved by passing the limit. There is an intersection between a person and inert matter; this intersection is a human being at the moment of death, when the circumstances preceding the death have been brutal to the point of making a thing of that person. This is a slave dying, a miserable bit of flesh nailed upon a cross.

If this slave is God, if he is the Second Person of the Trinity, if he is united to the First Person by the divine bond which is the Third Person, one has the perfection of harmony as the Pythagoreans conceived it, harmony in which is found the maximum distance and the maximum unity between the contraries. 'The common thought of separate thinkers.' There can be no thought that is more *one* than the thought of the unique God. There can be no thinking beings more separate than the Father and the Son at the moment when the Son emits that eternal cry: 'My God, my God, why hast thou forsaken me?' This moment is the incomprehensible perfection of love. It is the love which passes all understanding.

The ontological proof, the proof by perfection, which furthermore, is not a proof for the intelligence as such but only for the intelligence animated by love, this proof not only establishes

God's reality but also the reality of the dogmas of the Trinity, of the Incarnation and of the Passion. This certainty does not mean that the dogmas could have been found by human intelligence without revelation. But once the dogmas have appeared, they impose themselves upon the intelligence, if it is illumined by love, with such certainty that it cannot refuse to adhere, even though these dogmas are out of its domain and the intelligence is not qualified to affirm or to deny them. God is not perfect except as Trinity, and the love which constitutes the Trinity finds its perfection only in the Cross.

God wished to give His Son many brothers. The Pythagorean definition of friendship applies wonderfully to our friendship with God and to friendships between men.

'Friendship is an equality made of harmony.' If one takes harmony in the sense of geometric mean, if one conceives that the only mediation between God and man is a being at once God and man, one passes directly from this Pythagorean equation to the marvellous precepts of the Gospel of St. John. By assimilation with the Christ, who is one with God, the human being, lying in the depths of his misery, attains a sort of equality with God, an equality which is love. St. John of the Cross, speaking of the spiritual marriage, with the authority of experience, constantly repeats that, in the supreme union, God wishes to establish by love, between the soul and Himself, a sort of equality. St. Augustine also says: 'God was made man to the end that man might be made God.' Harmony is the principle of this sort of equality, harmony which is the bond between the contraries, the proportional mean, the Christ. It is not directly between God and man that there is something analogous to a bond of equality, it is between two relationships.

When Plato, in the *Gorgias*, speaks of geometric equality, this expression is doubtless exactly equivalent to that of harmonious equality employed by Pythagoras. Both terms constitute without doubt technical expressions whose meaning was rigorously defined by the equality between two ratios having a common term, of the type $\frac{a}{b} = \frac{b}{c}$. For the adjective geometric, in such terms as geometric mean and geometric progression, indicates proportion. The phrases from St. John cited above have so clearly and insistently the aspect of an algebraic equation that this is manifestly what is meant and what allusion is made to. Plato could certainly and legitimately say: 'Geometric equality has a great power both over the gods and over men.' Following the definition of friendship, the other expression from the same passage, 'Friendship unites heaven and earth, the gods and men', has exactly the same meaning. By inscribing over the door of his school 'Let no one enter who is not a geometer', Plato was doubtless affirming in the form of an enigma, and therefore as a pun, the truth which the Christ expressed in the saying, 'No one cometh unto the Father except by me.' The other Platonic equation, 'God is a perpetual geometer', obviously has a double sense and refers at the same time to the order of the world and to the mediatory function of the Word. To sum up, the appearance of geometry in Greece is the most dazzling of all the prophecies which foretold the Christ. One can thus understand how science, by its infidelity, should have become partly involved in the principle of evil, just as the devil entered Judas when he took bread from Christ's hand. Indifferent things remain forever indifferent; it is the divine things which, by refusing love, acquire diabolic efficacy. In the indifference which, since the Renaissance, science has shown for the spiritual life, there seems to be something diabolic. It would be vain to try to remedy this by an attempt to maintain science in the realm of nature alone. It is false that science belongs wholly to that domain. It belongs to it only by its results and practical applications, but not by its inspiration; for in science, as in art, all true novelty is the work of genius; and true genius, unlike talent, is supernatural. Neither does science belong to the domain of nature by its action upon the soul, for it confirms in faith or diverts from faith and cannot be indifferent to it. If it should again become faithful to its origin and its destination, demonstrative rigour in mathematics would be to Charity what musical technique is to Charity in the Gregorian melodies. There is a higher degree of musical technique in Gregorian plainsong than in Bach and Mozart themselves; the Gregorian chant is at once pure technique and pure love, in which, moreover, it is like all great art. It must be exactly the same for science, which, like art, is nothing but a special reflection of the beauty of the world. So it was in Greece. Demonstrative rigour is the material of the art of geometry as stone is the material of sculpture.

The Pythagorean definition of friendship, applied to God and to man, makes mediation appear as being essentially love, and love as being essentially the mediator. It is this also which Plato expresses in the *Symposium*.

The same definition applies also to friendship between men, although there is more difficulty in this since as Philolaus said: 'Things of the same species, of the same root, and of the same station, have no need of harmony.' It is significant that the Pythagoreans should have chosen a definition of friendship which does not apply to relationships between men except in the last place. Friendship is first friendship in God between the divine Persons. From this follows friendship between God and man. In the last place only is it friendship between two men or more. This hierarchy does not prevent human friendship from having existed among the Pythagoreans in its perfection, since the most celebrated pair of friends, Damon and Pythias, were of their number. Aristotle was doubtless inspired by the Pythagorean tradition in placing friendship among the virtues. If Iamblichus has not over-exaggerated, the Pythagoreans recognized, and applied among themselves to an admirable degree, a commandment similar to the last which Christ left to his disciples: 'Love one another.'

The Pythagorean definition applies to men, because although they are in fact of the same species, of the same root, of the same rank, they are not so in their thought. For each man, himself is I and all others are the others. I, that is to say, the centre of the world; that central position is represented in space by perspective. The others, that is to say those portions of the universe more or less important according as they are more or less near to I, are for the most part of no importance. It may happen that a man transfers the central position outside himself, into another human being, known or unknown to him personally, in whom he places his treasure and his heart. He himself then becomes a mere portion of the universe, sometimes fairly considerable, sometimes infinitely small. Extreme fear may produce this effect as well as a certain sort of love. In the two cases, when a human being finds the centre of the universe in another, this transference is always the effect of a combination of mechanical forces which brutally subject the first to the second. The effect occurs if the combination of forces is such that all thought of the future in the first, questions of hope and fear, pass necessarily through the second. There is an essential identity in the brutal and mechanical character of subordination in relationships apparently so different, which bind a slave to a master, a needy person to a benefactor, an old soldier to Napoleon, a certain type of lover, a father, a mother, a sister, a friend, and so on, to the object of their affection. A relation of this sort may link two human beings for a short space of time, a month, a day, a few minutes.

Except the cases where one human being is brutally subjected to another, who deprives him for a time of the power of thinking in the first person, everyone disposes of others as he disposes of inert things, either in fact, if he has the power, or in thought. There is, however, still one more exception. This is when two human beings meet in such circumstances that neither is subject to the other and each has to an equal degree need of the consent of the other. Each one then, without ceasing to think in the first person, really understands that the other also thinks in the first person. Justice then occurs as a natural phenomenon. The legislator's aim must be to make these occasions as numerous as possible. But the justice thus produced does not constitute harmony, and it is a justice without friendship. A formula which

Thucydides puts in the mouth of some Athenians perfectly defines the natural relations between human beings. 'The human mind being made as it is, the justice of a matter is examined only if there is an equal necessity on both sides. Contrarily, if one is strong and the other weak, what is possible is accomplished by the first and accepted by the second.' He adds: 'Of the gods, we believe, as of man, we certainly know, that it is a necessary law of their nature to rule wherever they can.'

Outside those occasions where there is equal need on both sides, justice is a supernatural friendship which results from harmony. Harmony is the unity of contraries. The contraries are God and man; that being which is the centre of the world, and that other which is a tiny fragment in the world. There can be unity only if, for all that it embraces, thought accomplishes an operation analogous to that which permits the perception of space by pushing back the illusions of perspective to their true position. It must be recognized that nothing in the world is the centre of the world, that the centre of the world is outside the world, that nothing here below has the right to say *I*. One must renounce in favour of God, through love for Him and for the truth, this illusory power which He has accorded us, to think in the first person. He has accorded it to us that it may be possible for us to renounce it by love. God alone has the right to say 'I am'; 'I am' is His name, and is the name of no other being. But this renunciation does not consist in transporting one's own position from the centre of the world into God as certain people transport it into another man. This would be to love God as Racine's Oenone loves Phèdre, as his Pylade loves Oreste. Some love God thus. Even though they should die as martyrs, theirs is not the veritable love of God. The 'I am' of God, which is real, differs infinitely from the illusory 'I am' of men. God is not a person in the way that a man believes himself to be. Here, doubtless, is the meaning of that profound Hindu saying that God must be conceived of as personal and impersonal at the same time.

Only the true renunciation of the power to think of everything in the first person, the renunciation which is not a simple transference, grants to a man the knowledge that other men are his fellows. This renunciation is the love of God, whether or not the name of God be present in the mind. This is why the two commandments make but one. In law, the love of God is first. But in fact, as among men all concrete thought has a real object, this renunciation necessarily operates while thought is applied either to things or to men. In the first case the love of God appears first as an adherence to the beauty of the world, the Stoic *amor fati*, the adherence to that indiscriminate distribution of the light and of the rain which here below expresses the perfection of our Heavenly Father. In the second case, the love of God appears first as love for one's neighbour, and before all for the weak and unfortunate neighbour, whom, according to the laws of nature, we do not even notice in passing near him. For the rest, just as true compassion is supernatural, so is true gratitude.

The renunciation of the power to think in the first person is the abandonment of all worldly goods in order to follow the Christ. All of a man's treasure is simply the whole universe seen with himself as its centre. Men only love riches, power and social consideration because they reinforce the faculty of thought in the first person. To accept poverty in the literal sense of the word, as St. Francis did, is to accept being nothing in the appearance which one presents to oneself and to others, just as one *is* nothing in reality. 'If a man would make himself invisible, there is no means more certain than to become poor,' say as Spanish folksong. Such an acceptance is the highest degree of love and of truth.

When one applies the formula 'Friendship is an equality made of harmony' to men, harmony has the meaning of the unity of contraries. The contraries are myself and the other, contraries so distant that they have their unity only in God. Friendship between human beings, and justice, are one and the same thing, except in the case where justice is imposed from outside by circumstances. Plato also, in the *Symposium*, indicates this identity between perfect justice and love. The Gospels use interchangeably the words justice and love with the same signification when it is a question of the relations between men; the word justice is used there several times in reference to alms. Those whom the Christ thanks for having given Him to eat when He was hungry, are called the just. Two perfect friends are two men who, being in frequent contact during a considerable portion of their lives, are always perfectly just one toward the other. An act of justice is a lightning flash of friendship which a fleeting opportunity causes to surge up between two men. If there is unilateral justice, it is one which is maimed.

In each of the three relationships indicated by the word friendship, God is always mediator. He is mediator between himself and himself. He is mediator between himself and man. He is mediator between one man and another. God is essentially mediation. God is the unique principle of harmony. This is why song is appropriate for his praise.

In saying: 'Where two or three are gathered together in my name, there am I in the midst of them,' Christ promised His friends, by extension, the infinitely precious good fortune of human friendship. But at whatever point in space and in time two real friends are to be found, an extremely rare thing, the Christ is among them no matter what may be the name of the God whom they invoke. All true friendship comes from the Christ.

However, there is a sort of renunciation of personality and a sort of friendship where the Christ is never present, even if He is explicitly and passionately invoked. This happens when one renounces the first person singular only to substitute the first person plural. Then the related terms are no longer myself and the other, or even myself and the others, but homogeneous fragments of us. These terms are thus of the same kind, of the same root, of the same rank; it follows then by Philolaus' postulate, that they cannot be joined together by harmony. They are joined by themselves and without mediation. There is no distance between them, no empty space between them where

God might enter. Nothing is more contrary to friendship than solidarity, be it a question of solidarity based on comradeship, personal sympathy, or membership in a common social group, or the same political conviction, the same nation, the same religious confession. The thoughts which, explicitly or implicitly, enclose the first person plural are infinitely further removed from justice than those which enclose the first person singular; for the first person plural is not susceptible of being involved in a relationship in three terms of which the middle term is God. This is why Plato, very probably inspired by the Pythagoreans, called everything collective, animal. This trap for love is the most dangerous of all that are set here below. Innumerable Christians have fallen into this trap in the course of the centuries, they fall into it even in our day.

Supernatural justice, supernatural friendship or love, are found to be implicit in all human relationships where, without there being an equality of force or of need, there is a search for mutual consent. The desire for mutual consent is charity. This is an imitation of the incomprehensible charity which persuades God to allow us our autonomy.

Besides that of the Trinity, of the Incarnation, of the charity between God and man, and of the charity between men, there is a fifth form of harmony, which concerns things. This also surrounds man in so far as a man is a thing, that is to say, the whole man, body and soul, except the faculty of free consent. It proceeds to englobe what each one calls myself. This fifth form of harmony, not being concerned with persons, does not constitute a friendship. The contraries to which it is related are the principle which limits, and that which receives limits from outside, which is to say: God and inert matter as such. The intermediary is the limit, the network of limits, which hold all things in a single order and of which Lao Tsu has said: 'The net of the heavens is very large, but none can pass through it.'

The idea of this pair of contraries is not evident, it is even at first very obscure. It is also very profound. It comprises all the great constructions that have been made throughout the centuries under the name of theories of knowledge.

It is number, says Philolaus, which gives things a body. He adds that number accomplishes this effect by making them understandable as is provided by the nature of the gnomon. The word gnomon, if taken in its first sense, is the vertical stem of the sundial. This stem remains immobile while its shadow turns and changes in length. The variableness of the shadow is determined by the immobility of the stem on account of the movement of the turning sun. This relationship is the one which mathematicians today refer to by the names of the invariant and the group of variation. This is one of the fundamental ideas of the human mind.

It is surprising to read that number gives a body to things. We would sooner expect a form. Yet Philolaus' formula is literally true. All concise and rigorous analysis of perception, of illusion, of fantasy, of dream, of those states more or less near to hallucination, show that the perception of the real world differs from the errors resembling it, only because the real includes a contact with necessity. (Maine de Biran, Lagneau and Alain have shown the greatest discernment upon this point.) Necessity always appears to us as an ensemble of laws of variation, determined by fixed relationships and invariants. Reality for the human mind is contact with necessity. There is a contradiction here, for necessity is intelligible, not tangible. Thus the feeling of reality constitutes a harmony and a mystery. We convince ourselves of the reality of an object by going around it, an operation successively producing varied appearances which are determined by the immobility of a form which is different from all the appearances, exterior to them and transcending them. By this operation we know that the object is a thing and not an apparition, that it has a body.

Thus quantitative relationships which play the part of the gnomon do indeed constitute the body of the object. Lagneau, to whom Philolaus' equation was doubtless unknown, made this analysis by means of a cubic box. None of the appearances (or views) of the box has the form of a cube, but whoever turns the box around knows that the cubic form is what determines the variation of the apparent form. This determining factor constitutes the very body of the object so well for us, that in looking at the box we believe we see a cube, which, however, is never the case. The relationship of the cube, which, properly speaking, is never seen in the appearances produced by perspective, is like the relationship of the stem of the sundial to the shadows. The example of the cube is perhaps still more beautiful. Either one of these relationships can, by an analogical transposition, furnish the key to the whole of human knowledge. There is great profit in meditating indefinitely upon these relationships.

For us the reality of the universe is necessity whose structure is that of the gnomon, supported by something. Necessity must have a support, for by itself it is essentially conditional. Without a basis, it is but abstraction; upon a basis it constitutes the reality of creation itself. Of that basis we cannot have the least conception. However the Greeks had a word (ἄπειρον), which means at once unlimited and indeterminate. This is what Plato calls the receptacle, the matrix, the hallmark, the essence which is the mother of all things and at the same time always intact, always virginal. Water is the best image of this because it has neither form nor colour even though it be visible and tangible. On this subject it is impossible not to notice that the words matter, mother, sea (*mer*), Marie resemble each other to the point of being almost identical. This character of water takes into account its symbolic use in baptism more than its power to wash.

For us, matter is simply what is subjected to necessity. We know nothing else about it. Necessity is constituted for us by the quantitative laws of variation in the appearances. Where there is, strictly speaking, no quantity, there is something analogous; a quantitative law of variation, that is a function. Function is what the Greeks called number or relationship, *arithmos* or *logos*, and it is also this which constitutes limit. The clearest image of function is furnished by a continuous series of triangles having the same angles. This is a proportion. It is by geometry that the idea of function is revealed.

Necessity is an enemy for man as long as he thinks in the first person. To tell the truth, he has with necessity the three sorts of relationship which he has with men. In fantasy, or by the exercise of social power, it seems to be his slave. In adversities, privations, grief, sufferings, but above all in affliction, it seems an absolute and brutal master. In methodical action there is a point of equilibrium where necessity, by its conditional character, presents man at once with obstacles and with means in relation to the partial ends which he pursues and wherein there is a sort of equality between a man's will and universal necessity. This point of equilibrium is to the relationships of man with the world what natural justice is to the relationships between men. In the organization of work, of technology, of all human activity, one must, try to achieve this point of equilibrium as often as possible. For the particular task of the legislator is to create in social life, to the full measure of the possible, natural images of supernatural virtues. This active equilibrium between man and universal necessity, joined to the equilibrium of forces and of needs between men, would constitute, if such a thing could exist for a long time, natural happiness. The aspiration to natural happiness is good, healthy and precious; just as it is good for the health of a child that he should be attracted to food by its savour, although the chemical composition, and not the savour, constitutes the good in it. The experience of, and the desire for, supernatural joys do not destroy the soul's aspiration to natural happiness, they confer a fullness and a significance upon it. Natural happiness has no real value except when a perfectly pure joy is added to it by the sentiment of beauty. Crime and affliction, each one in a different manner but with equal efficacy, destroy forever the aspiration to natural joy.

The equilibrium between the human will and necessity in methodical action is only an image; if one takes it for a reality it is a lie. Notably what man takes for his ends are always simply his means. Fatigue forces him to find illusion. In the state of intense fatigue, man ceases to cling to his own action and even to his own will; he sees himself as a thing which pushes others because it is itself pushed by a constraint. Effectually, the human will, although a certain sentiment of choice be irreducibly attached to it, is simply a phenomenon among all those which are subject to necessity. The proof of this is that the will admits limits. The infinite alone is outside the empire of necessity.

In the universe, man experiences necessity only so far as it is at once an obstacle and a condition of accomplishing his will. Henceforth the experience of necessity is never entirely free of illusions inevitably connected with the exercise of the will. To think of necessity in a way that is pure, it must be detached from the matter which supports it and conceived as a fabric of conditions knotted one with the others. Necessity, both pure and conditional, is the true object of mathematics and of certain operations of thought which are analogous to mathematics; which are as theoretical, pure, and rigorous as mathematics but which are not given a name because they are not discerned. Contrary to a quite widespread prejudice of our day, mathematics is before all a science of nature; or rather, it is *the* science of nature, the only one. Every other science is simply a particular application of mathematics.

If necessity is thought of as conditional, man is not present under any heading, he has no part in it outside the very process by which he thinks it. The faculty from which this procceeds is understood by its nature to be withdrawn from necessity, withdrawn from limit and from number. The purely conditional progression of necessity is the progression of demonstration itself. Thus regarded, necessity is for man no longer either an enemy or a master. And yet it is something strange and which imposes its presence. The knowledge of sensible phenomena is uniquely the recognition in these phenomena of something analogous to that purely conditional necessity. The same is true for psychological and social phenomena. One knows them so far as one recognizes in them, concretely and precisely at each occasion, the presence of a necessity analogous to mathematical necessity. This is why the Pythagoreans said that we know nothing but number. They called mathematical necessity number or relationship (λόγος or λογισμός).

Mathematical necessity is an intermediary between the whole natural part of man which is corporeal and psychical matter and the infinitely small portion of himself which does not belong to this world. Man, though he struggles, often vainly, to sustain in himself the contrary illusion, is here below the slave of natural forces which infinitely surpass him. This force which governs the world and makes every man obey, as a man armed with a lash is certain to make a slave obey, this force is the same as that which the human mind conceives of under the name of necessity. The relationship of necessity to the intelligence is not the relationship of the master to the slave. Neither is it the reverse, nor that of two free men. It is the relationship of the object contemplated to the contemplation. The faculty in man which looks upon the most brutal force, as one looks at a picture, naming it necessity, is not the portion of man which belongs to the other world. That faculty is at the intersection of the two worlds. The faculty which does not belong to this world is the faculty of consent. Man is free to consent to necessity, or not. This liberty is not actual in him except when he conceives of force as necessity, that is to say, when he contemplates it. He is not free to consent to force as such. The slave who sees the lash lifted above him does not consent, nor refuse his consent, he trembles. And yet under the name of necessity it is indeed to brute force that man consents, and when he consents it is indeed to a lash. No mover, no motive can be sufficient for such a consent. This consent is madness, man's own particular madness, the madness that belongs to man, like Creation, like the Incarnation, together with the Passion, constitute God's own madness. These two madnesses answer each other. It is not surprising that this world should be the place of affliction above all other, for without perpetually suspended disaster no folly on man's part could echo that of God, which is already wholly contained in the act of creation. For in creating God renounces being all, He abandons a bit of being to what is other than Himself. Creation is renunciation by love. The true response to the excess of divine love does not consist in voluntarily inflicting suffering upon oneself, for the suffering one inflicts upon oneself, however intense or long, or violent it may be, is not destructive. It is not in the power of a being to destroy himself. The true reply consists only in consenting to the possibility of being destroyed, that is to say, in the possibility of total disaster, whether that disaster actually happens or not. No one ever inflicts disaster on himself, neither out of love nor perversity. At the most one can, under one or the other inspiration, take distractedly and as if unconsciously two or three steps leading to the slippery point where one becomes a prey to gravity and from which one falls on stones that break one's back.

The consent to necessity is pure love, and even in a certain manner an excess of love. This love has not necessity itself for object, nor the visible world of which it is the stuff. It is not in man's power to love matter as such. When a man loves an object, it is either because he has in thought lodged a portion of his past life in it, sometimes also a desired future, or else because this object refers to another human being. One loves an object which is a reminder of a beloved person, or a work of art which is the work of a man of genius. The universe is a memento for us; the reminder of some beloved being? The universe is a work of art; what artist is the author of it? We have no answers to these questions. But when love, from which the consent to necessity proceeds, exists in us, we possess experimental proof that there is an answer. For it is not out of love for other men that we consent to necessity. The love for other men is in a sense an obstacle to this consent, for necessity crushes those others as well as ourselves. It is for the love of something which is not a human person, and who is yet something like a person. For what is not something like a person is not an object of love. Whatever a person's professed belief in regard to religious matters, including atheism, wherever there is complete, authentic and unconditional consent to necessity, there is fullness of love for God; and nowhere else. This consent constitutes participation in the Cross of Christ.

In naming *Logos* that human and divine being whom he loved above all and by whom he was cherished, St. John included in one word, among several other infinitely precious thoughts, the whole Stoic doctrine of *amor fati*. This word *Logos*, borrowed from the Greek Stoics who had received it from Heraclitus, has several meanings, but the principal one is that quantitative law of variation which constitutes necessity. *Fatum* and *logos* are, moreover, semantically related. *Fatum* is necessity, necessity is the *logos*, and *logos* is the real name of what we most ardently love. The love which St. John bore for Him who was his friend and his Lord when he was leaning on His bosom during the Last Supper, is the same love which we should bear toward the mathematical progression of causes and effects which, from time to time, make of us a sort of formless jelly. This is manifestly absurd.

One of Christ's most profound and most obscure sayings reveals this absurdity. The bitterest reproach that men make of this necessity is its absolute indifference to moral values. Righteous men and criminals receive an equal share of the benefits of the sun and of the rain; the righteous and the criminals equally suffer sunstroke, and drowning in floods. It is precisely this indifference which the Christ invites us to look upon and to imitate as the very expression of the perfection of our heavenly Father. To imitate this indifference is simply to consent to it, that is, to accept the existence of all that exists, including the evil, excepting only that portion of evil which we have the possibility, and the obligation, of preventing. By this simple word the Christ annexed all Stoic thought, and by the same token all of Heraclitus and Plato.

No one could ever prove that such an absurdity as consent to necessity could be possible. We can only recognize it. There are in fact souls which consent to it.

Necessity is precisely the intermediary between our nature and our infinitely small faculty of free consent, for our nature is submissive to it and our consent accepts it. Even so, when we think of the universe, we think also of necessity as being the intermediary between matter and God. As we consent to necessity, so first of all God, by an eternal act, consents to it. But what in ourselves we call consent, in God we call His Will. God causes the existence of necessity to be spread throughout space and time by the fact that He thinks it. God's thought is God, and in this sense the Son is the image of the Father. God's thought is also the order of the world, and in this sense the Word is the orderer of the world, for in God all is subject, all is person.

Just as the Christ is, on one hand, the mediator between God and man, and on the other the mediator between man and his neighbour, so mathematical necessity is on one hand the mediator between God and things, and on the other between each thing and every other thing. This necessity constitutes an order whereby each thing, being in its place, permits all other things to exist. The maintenance of boundaries constitutes for material things the equivalent of what the consent to the existence of others is for the human spirit, that is to say charity toward one's neighbour. Moreover, for man, in so far as he is a natural being, keeping within limits is justice.

Order is equilibrium and immobility. The universe, submissive to time, is a perpetual becoming. The energy which moves it is the principle of rupture of equilibrium. But, nevertheless, this becoming, composed of the ruptures of equilibrium, is in reality an equilibrium because the ruptures of equilibrium compensate each other. This becoming is equilibrium refracted in time. This is what Anaximander's prodigious formula expresses, that formula of unfathomable depth: 'It is starting from the indeterminate that the birth of things is accomplished. It is by a return to the indeterminate that their destruction comes about in conformity with necessity. For they submit to a chastisement and make reparation to each other, because of their injustice, according to the order of time.' Considered in itself all change, and consequently any phenomenon, however small, includes the principle of the destruction of universal order. Conversely, considered in its connection with all phenomena contained in the totality of space and of time, connection which imposes a limit upon change and puts it in relation to an equal and inverse rupture of equilibrium, each phenomenon contains in itself the total presence of the order of the world.

Necessity being the mediator between matter and God, we conceive of God's will with regard to necessity, and with regard to matter, as being two different relationships. For the human imagination this difference is expressed in an inevitably defective manner by the myth of the original chaos wherein God establishes an order; ancient wisdom was wrongly reproached for this myth, of which a trace is also found in Genesis. Another manner of indicating this difference is to relate necessity particularly to the Second Person of the Trinity, regarded either as orderer, or as the Soul of the World. The Soul of the World is the order of the world conceived of as a person. An Orphic verse indicates the same difference by saying: 'Zeus created the universe and Bacchus completed it.' Bacchus is the Word. Even though matter exists only in that it is willed by God, necessity, being mediator, is nearer to God's will. Necessity is the obedience of matter to God. Thus the pair of contraries constituted by necessity in matter, and liberty in us, has its meeting in obedience, for to be free, for us, is to desire to obey God. All other liberty is false.

When things are thus conceived of, the idea of a miracle is no longer one which we can accept or refuse; it has, rigorously, no least significance. Or rather, it has no other significance than that of an appearance exercising a certain influence upon souls at a certain level, a mixed influence of good and of evil.

So long as we think in the first person, we see necessity from below, from inside, it encloses us on all sides as the surface of the earth and the arc of the sky. From the time we renounce thinking in the first person, by consent to necessity, we see it from outside, beneath us for we have passed to God's side. The side which it turned to us before, and still presents to almost the whole of our being, the natural part of ourselves, is brute domination. The side which it presents after this operation, to the fragment of our mind which has passed to the other side, is pure obedience. We have become sons of the home, and we love the docility of this slave, necessity, which at first we took for a master.

But the possibility of such a change in point of view is inconceivable without experience. At the moment when we are resolved to consent to necessity, we cannot foresee the fruits of this consent. This consent is truly in the first place pure absurdity. Also it is truly supernatural. It is the work of Grace alone. God works in us without us if only we allow ourselves to be worked upon. When we become conscious of this, the work is already done, we find ourselves pledged without ever having taken a pledge; we can no longer turn away from God except by an act of high treason.

As a horizontal place is the unity of the upper and of the lower surfaces, necessity is for matter the intersection of obedience to God and of the brute force which subdues creatures. At this same level of the intersection, necessity participates in constraint on the one hand, and on the other participates in intelligence, in justice, in beauty and in faith. The share in constraint is evident. There is for example something hard, metallic, opaque, something irreducible by the mind in the connection between the different properties of the triangle and of the circle.

But just as the order of the world, in God, is a divine Person which may be called the ordering Word, or the Soul of the World, so in us, the younger brothers, necessity is relationship —that is to say, thought in action. 'The eyes of the soul,' says Spinoza 'are the demonstrations themselves.' It is not in our power to modify the sum of the squares of the sides in the right-angled triangle, but there is no sum if the mind does not work it out by conceiving the demonstration. Already in the domain of whole numbers, one and one can remain side by side throughout perpetuity of time; they never will make two unless an intelligence performs the act of adding them. Attentive intelligence alone has the power of carrying out the connections, and as soon as that attention relaxes, the connections dissolve. Doubtless there are in us very many connections belonging to the memory, to the sensibility, to the imagination, to habit, to belief; but these do not include necessity. The necessary connections which constitute the very reality of the world have no reality in themselves except as the object of intellectual attention in action. This correlation between necessity and the free act of the attention is a marvel. The greater the indispensable effort of attention, the more this marvel is visible. That is much more obvious in regard to funda-mental truths concerning quantities called irrational, such as the square root of two, than in regard to fundamental truths concern-ing whole numbers. To conceive of the first with the same rigour as of the second, to conceive of them as rigorously necessary, requires a much greater effort of attention. Also they are much more precious.

This virtue of intellectual attention makes it an image of the Wisdom of God. God creates by the act of thinking. We, by intellectual attention, do not indeed create, we produce no object, yet in our sphere we do in a certain way give birth to reality.

This intellectual attention is at the intersection of the natural and of the supernatural part of the soul. Having conditional necessity as object, this attention produces only a half-reality. We confer upon objects and upon persons around us all that we have of the fullness of reality when to this intellectual attention we add that attention of still higher degree which is acceptance, consent, love. But already the fact that the relationship which makes up the tissue of necessity is dependent upon the act of our attention makes it a thing belonging to us which we can love. Also every human being who suffers is somewhat relieved, if only he has a certain elevation of spirit, when he clearly perceives the necessary connection of causes and effects which produce his suffering.

Necessity shares also in justice. And yet in a sense it is the contrary of justice. We have understood nothing so long as we do not know what difference there is, as Plato says, between the essence of the necessary and that of the good. Justice for man presents itself first as a choice, choice of the good, rejection of evil. Necessity is the absence of choice, indifference. Yet it is the principle of coexistence. And basically the supreme justice for us is acceptance of the coexistence with ourselves of all creatures and all things which make up the existent. It is permissible to have enemies, but not to desire that they should not exist. If a man truly has no such desire, he will do nothing to put an end to their existence. Outside the strictly obligatory cases one will do them no harm. Nothing more is required if it is well understood that to abstain from the good which one has the opportunity to do a human being, is to do him harm. If we accept the coexistence with ourselves of beings and of things, we shall not be avid for domination or riches, since domination and riches have no other use than to cast a veil over this coexistence, diminishing the share of all that is other than ourselves. All crimes, all grave sins are particular forms of the refusal of this coexistence; a sufficiently close analysis shows this for each particular case.

There is an analogy between the fidelity of the right-angled triangle to the relationship which forbids it to emerge from the circle of which its hypotenuse is the diameter, and that of a man who, for example, abstains from the acquisition of power or of money at the price of fraud. The first may be regarded as a perfect example of the second. One can say as much, when one has perceived mathematical necessity in nature, of the fidelity of floating bodies in rising out of water precisely as much as their density exacts, no more and no less. Heraclitus says: 'The sun shall not go beyond its boundaries; otherwise the Erinyes, servants of Justice would overtake it *in flagrante delicto*.' There is an incorruptible fidelity in things to their place in the order of the world, fidelity to which man may present his equivalent only once he has arrived at perfection, once become identical with his own vocation. The contemplation of the fidelity of things, either in the visible world, or in their mathematical relationships, or analogies, is a powerful means of achieving that fidelity. The first lesson of this contemplation is not to choose but to consent impartially to the existence of all that exists. This universal consent is the same thing as detachment, and any attachment, even the weakest and most legitimate in appearance, is an obstacle to it. This is why it must never be forgotten that the light shines impartially on all beings and things. It is thus the image of the creative will of God which upholds equally all that exists. It is to this creative will that our consent must adhere.

It is the beauty of the world which permits us to contemplate and to love necessity. Without beauty this would not be possible. For even though this consent is the very function of the supernatural part of the soul, it cannot in fact operate without a certain complicity from the natural part of the soul and even of the body. The fullness of this complicity is the fullness of joy; extreme unhappiness on the contrary makes this complicity, at least for a time, absolutely impossible. But even those men who have the infinitely precious privilege of participation in the Cross of Christ could not attain to it if they had not been through joy. The Christ knew the perfection of human joy before being precipitated to the depth of human distress. And pure joy is nothing but the feeling of beauty.

Beauty is a mystery; it is what is most mysterious here below. But it is a fact. Everybody recognizes its power, including the most worn or the most vile, although very few know how to understand and to use it. It is invoked in the lowest debauchery. In a general manner, all human beings use words that refer to beauty to designate all the things they rightly or wrongly give value to, whatever the nature of the value might be. One might believe that they regard beauty as the supreme value.

To be precise, there is here below but one single beauty,

that is the Beauty of the World. All other beauties are reflections of that one, be they faithful and pure, deformed and soiled, or even diabolically perverted.

In fact, the world is beautiful. When we are alone in the heart of nature and disposed to give it attention, something inclines us to love what surrounds us, which, however, consists only of brute matter, inert, dumb and deaf. And beauty touches us all the more keenly where necessity appears in a most manifest manner, for example in the folds that gravity has impressed upon the mountains, on the waves of the sea, or on the course of the stars. In pure mathematics also, necessity is resplendent in beauty.

Doubtless the very essence of the perception of beauty is itself the sentiment of that necessity one of whose facets is brutal constraint and the other obedience to God. Thanks to a providential mercy, this truth is made manifest in the carnal part of our soul, and even in some sort to our bodies.

This cluster of marvels is perfected by the presence, in the necessary connections which compose the universal order, of divine verities symbolically expressed. Herein is the marvel of marvels, and as it were, the secret signature of the artist.

One does double harm to mathematics when one regards it only as a rational and abstract speculation. It is that, but it is also the very science of nature, a science totally concrete, and it is also a mysticism, those three together and inseparably.

When one contemplates the property which makes of the circle the locus of the apices of the right-angled triangles having the same hypotenuse, if one pictures at the same time a point describing the circle and the projection of this point upon the diameter, contemplation may extend far toward the depth and toward the height. The affinity of the movements of the two points, one circular, the other alternating, includes the possibility of all the transformations of circular movements into alternating ones, and conversely, which are the bases of our technology. This is the principle of the operation by which a grinder sharpens knives.

On the other hand, the circular movement, if one conceives

not of a point but a whole circle turning upon itself, is the perfect image of the eternal act which constitutes the life of the Trinity. This movement constitutes one operation without any change and which curves upon itself. The alternating movement of the point which comes and goes upon the diameter enclosed by the circle, is the image of all becoming here below; an image made of successive and contrary ruptures of equilibrium, the equivalent variant of a motionless equilibrium in action. This becoming is indeed the projection of divine life upon earth. As the circle encloses the moving point upon the diameter, God assigns a term to all the becomings of this world. As the Bible says, He rules the raging of the sea. The segment on the right angle which joins the point of the circle to its projection upon the diameter is, in the figure, an intermediary between the circle and the diameter. At the same time, from the point of view of quantities, it is, like the mean proportional, the mediation between the two parts of the diameter which are on either side of the point. This is the image of the Word. In a general way the circle is necessary to the construction of any proportional mean between quantities whose relationship is not a rational number to the second power. And the mean is always furnished by a perpendicular joining a point of the circle to the diameter. If one extends the perpendicular on the other side, one has a cross inscribed in a circle. If the terms between which a mean is sought are in the relation of one to two, it is demonstrable that no whole number can furnish the solution because this must be at once even and odd. Thus one may say that the quantity which constitutes this mean, and which is the measure of this right-hand segment, is at once even and odd. The Pythagoreans considered the opposition between the odd and even as an image of the opposition between the supernatural and the natural, because of the kinship of the odd with unity. All this is contained in the act of a grinder, or of a dressmaker who moves a wheel by means of a pedal.

What we have here is only a small example. In a general way, and in the widest sense, mathematics, including under this name all rigorous and pure theoretical study of necessary relationships, constitutes at once the unique knowledge of the material universe wherein we exist and the clearest reflection of divine truths. No miracle, no prophecy is comparable to the marvel of this concordance. To conceive the extent of this marvel one must understand that the very perception of sensible things among human beings, even the least developed, contains implicitly a great many of mathematical relationships which are the condition of that perception; that even the most primitive technique is always to a certain degree applied mathematics, at least implicitly; that the methodical handling of mathematical relationships in the movements of work and technology alone can, now and then, give man this feeling of harmony with the forces of nature, which corresponds to natural happiness; that the use of these mathematical relationships alone permits one to consider the sensible world as being made up of inert matter, and not of numberless capricious divinities. It is this same mathematics which is first, before all, a sort of mystical poem composed by God himself. This is so wonderful that one is tempted to doubt that so great a matter should be so recent, and to suppose that perhaps the Greeks did not invent, but in part simply divulged, and in part rediscovered, geometry.

At the end of such meditations, one reaches an extremely simple view of the universe. God has created, that is, not that He has produced something outside Himself, but that He has withdrawn Himself, permitting a part of being to be other than God. To this divine renunciation, the renunciation of creation responds, that is to say, obedience, responds. The whole universe is a compact mass of obedience. This compact mass is sprinkled with points of light. Each one of these points is the supernatural part of the soul of a reasonable creature who loves God and who consents to obey. The rest of the soul is held in the compact mass. The beings gifted with reason who do not love God are only fragments of the compact and obscure mass. They also are wholly obedient but only in the manner of a falling stone. Their soul also is matter, psychic matter, humbled to a mechanism as rigorous as that of gravity. Even their belief in their own free arbitration, the illusions of their pride, their defiance, their revolts, are all simply phenomena as rigorously determined as the refraction of light. Considered thus, as inert matter, the worst criminals make up a part of the order of the world and therefore of the beauty of the world. Everything obeys God, therefore everything is perfect beauty. To know that, to know it really, is to be perfect as the heavenly Father is perfect.

This universal love belongs only to the contemplative faculty of the soul. He who truly loves God leaves its proper function to each part of his soul. Beneath the faculty of supernatural contemplation is found a part of the soul which is at the level of obligation and for which the opposition of good and evil must have all possible force. Still lower is the animal part of the soul, which must be methodically trained by a wise combination of whiplashes and lumps of sugar.

In those who love God, even in those who are perfect, the natural part of the soul is always entirely subject to mechanical necessity. But the presence of supernatural love in the soul constitutes a new factor of the mechanism and transforms it.

We are like shipwrecked persons clinging to logs upon the sea and tossed in an entirely passive manner by every movement of the waves. From the height of heaven God throws each one a rope. He who seizes the rope and does not let go, despite the pain and the fear, remains as much as the others subject to the buffeting of the waves; only for him these buffets combine with the tension of the cord to form a different mechanical whole.

Thus, although the supernatural does not descend into the domain of nature, nature is yet changed by the presence of the supernatural. The virtue which is common to all those who love God, and the most surprising miracles of certain saints, are likewise explained by this influence which is as mysterious as beauty and of the same species. Both are a reflection in nature of the supernatural.

When one conceives the universe as an immense mass of blind obedience sprinkled with points of consent, one conceives also one's own being as a little mass of blind obedience with a point of consent at the centre. The consent is supernatural love, it is the Spirit of God in us. The blind obedience is the inertia of matter, which is perfectly represented for our imagination by the element at once resistant and fluid, that is to say, by water. At the moment when we consent to obedience, we are born of water and of the spirit. We are henceforth a being composed uniquely of the spirit and of water.

The consent to obey is mediator between blind obedience and God. The perfect consent is that of the Christ. Our consent can only be a reflection of that of the Christ. The Christ is mediator between God and ourselves on one side, and on the other between God and the universe. Likewise we, in so far as it is granted us to imitate Christ, have this extraordinary privilege of being, to a certain degree, mediators between God and His own creation.

But the Christ is Mediation itself, and Harmony itself. Philolaus said: 'Things which are neither of the same species nor of the same nature, nor of the same station, have need to be locked together under key by a harmony capable of maintaining them in a universal order.' The Christ is that key which locks together the Creator and creation. Since knowledge is the reflection of being, the Christ is also, by that same token, the key of knowledge. 'Woe unto you, lawyers!' said he, 'for ye have taken away the key of knowledge.'[1] He was that key, He whom earlier centuries had loved in advance, and whom the Pharisees had denied and were going to put to death.

Grief, said Plato, is the dissolution of harmony, the separation of contraries; joy is their reunion. The crucifixion of the Christ has almost opened the door, has almost separated on one side the Father and the Son, on the other the Creator and creation. The door half-opened. The resurrection closed it again. Those who have the immense privilege of participating with their whole

---

[1] St. Luke xi, 52.

being in the Cross of Christ, go through that door, they pass to the side where the secrets of God Himself are to be found.

But more generally, every sort of grief, and above all every sort of disaster well endured, makes the passage to the other side of that door possible, makes the true face of harmony seen. That face which is turned toward the heights rends one of the veils which separate us from the beauty of the world and the beauty of God. This is what the end of the book of Job reveals. Job, at the end of his distress, which despite appearances he has perfectly well endured, receives the revelation of the beauty of the world.

There is, moreover, a sort of equivalence between joy and sorrow. Joy also is revelation of beauty. Everything carries that man forward who keeps his eyes ever fixed upon the key.

There are three mysteries in human life of which all human beings, even the most mediocre, have more or less knowledge. One is beauty. Another is the work of pure intelligence applied to the contemplation of theoretic necessity in the understanding of the world, and the incarnation of these purely theoretical conceptions in technique and in work. The last are those flashes of justice, of compassion, of gratitude which rise up sometimes in human relationships in the midst of harshness and metallic coldness. Here are three supernatural mysteries constantly present right in human nature. These are three openings which give direct access to the central door which is the Christ. Because of their presence there is no possibility of a profane or natural life being innocent for man here below. There is only faith, implicit or explicit, or else betrayal. One must come to see above the skies and throughout the universe nothing but divine mediation. God is mediation, and all mediation is God. God is mediation between God and God, between God and man, between man and man, between God and things, between things and things, and even between each soul and itself. One cannot pass from nothing to nothing without passing through God. God is the unique path. He is the Way. Way was His name in ancient China.

Man cannot understand this divine operation of mediation, he can only love it. But in a perfectly clear manner his intelligence conceives a degraded image of it, which is the relationship. There is never anything in human thought but relationships. Even where the objects of the senses are concerned, it becomes clear, as soon as one analyses the perception of them in a fairly strict manner, that what one calls objects are simply groups of relationships which impose themselves upon the mind by the intervention of the senses. It is the same with sentiments, ideas, and the whole psychological content of the human consciousness.

We have in us and about us only relationships. In the semi-darkness in which we are plunged, all is relation for us, as in the light of reality all is in itself divine mediation. Relationship is divine mediation glimpsed through our darkness.

This identity is what St. John expressed in giving to Christ the name of the relation, *logos*, and what the Pythagoreans expressed in saying: 'All is number.'

When we know that, we know that we live in divine mediation, not as a fish in the sea but as a drop of water in the sea. In us, outside us, here below, in the Kingdom of God, nowhere is there any other thing. And mediation is exactly the same thing as Love.

The supreme mediation is that of the Holy Spirit uniting through infinite distance the divine Father to the equally divine Son, but emptied of His divinity and nailed to a point in space and in time. This infinite distance is made of the totality of space and of time. The portion of space around us, bounded by the circle of the horizon, the portion of time between our birth and our death, which we live second after second, which is the stuff of our life, is a fragment of this infinite distance entirely pierced by divine love. The being and the life of each one of us are together a tiny segment of this line whose extremities are two Persons and a single God, this line where Love circulates is also that same God. We are a point through which God's divine Love for self passes. In no case are we anything else. But if we know this, and if we consent to it, all our being, all that in us appears to be ourselves, becomes infinitely more foreign, more indifferent, and more distant, than this uninterrupted passage of God's Love.

N.B.—It may appear surprising to find the Incarnation presented in these pages not as destined for men but as being, on the contrary, that to which the destiny of man is related. There is no incompatibility between these two inverse relationships. We speak above all of the first for an evident reason, that men are much more interested in themselves than in God. The second is shown in a very clear and definite manner by St. Paul's phrase: 'God wanted to give his Son many brothers.' This is perhaps still more true than the other order, for in everything God is prior to man in all respects. This perhaps gives a better account of the mysteries of human life. This terminology leads to a new insight into our destiny, and notably into the relations between suffering and sin. The effects of misfortune upon innocent souls are really unintelligible unless we remember that we have been created as brothers of the crucified Christ. The absolute domination throughout the whole universe of a mechanical, mathematical, absolutely deaf and blind necessity is unintelligble, unless one believes that the whole universe, in the totality of space and of time, has been created as the Cross of Christ. Here is the profound meaning, probably, of Christ's reply about the man born blind and the cause of his affliction.

The principal effect of affliction is to force the soul to cry out 'why', as did the Christ Himself, and to repeat this cry unceasingly, except when exhaustion interrupts it. There is no reply. When one finds a comforting reply, first of all one has constructed it oneself; then the fact that one has the power to construct it shows that the suffering, however intense it is, has not attained the specific degree of affliction, just as water does not boil at 99 degrees centigrade. If the word 'why' expressed the search for a cause, the reply would appear easily. But it expresses the search for an end. This whole universe is empty of finality. The soul which, because it is torn by affliction, cries out continually for this finality, touches the void. If it does not renounce loving, it happens one day to hear, not a reply to the question which it cries, for there is none, but the very silence as something infinitely more full of significance than any response, like God himself speaking. It knows then that God's absence here below is the same thing as the secret presence upon earth of the God who is in heaven. But to hear the divine silence one must have been forced to seek vainly for a finality, and two things only have the power to force one to that, either affliction, or pure joy which comes from the perception of beauty. Beauty has this power because although it contains no particular finality, it gives the imperious feeling of the presence of a finality. Affliction, and extreme and pure joy, are the only two ways and they are equivalent, but the way of affliction is the way of Christ.

The cry of the Christ and the silence of the Father together make the supreme harmony, that harmony of which all music is but an imitation, that to which our harmonies, those at once the most heartbreaking and the most sweet, bear an infinitely far away and dim resemblance. The whole universe, including our own existences as tiny fragments of it, is only the vibration of that harmony.

In all comparison of this sort, which seems to dissolve the reality of the universe in God's favour, there is danger of the error of pantheism. But the analysis of the perception of a cubic box gives a perfect metaphor in this regard, one prepared for us by God. There is no point of view from which the box has the appearance of a cube; one never sees more than flat sides; the angles do not seem straight, the sides do not seem equal. No one has ever seen, no one ever will see, a cube. Neither has anyone ever touched, nor ever will touch a cube, for analogous reasons. If one goes round the box, one engenders an indefinite variety of apparent forms. The cubic form is none of these. It is different from all of them, exterior to them all, transcending their domain. At the same time the cubic form constitutes their unity. It also constitutes their truth.

We know this so well with the whole soul, that by a sort of transference of the sense of reality, every time we see a box, we believe we see directly and really a cube. And still this expression is much too weak. We have the certainty of a contact, direct and real, between our thought and matter in the form of a cube.

Thus God, by so disposing the corporeal senses for our use, has given us a perfect model of the love we owe Him. He has included a revelation in our sensibility itself.

As in looking at the box from any point of view we no longer see all the acute or obtuse angles, the uneven lines, but only a cube, so in experiencing any event in the world, and no matter what state of soul in ourselves, we need hardly perceive them, but only see through them a single, fixed and unchanging order of the world. This order is not a mathematical form but a Person; and that Person is God.

As a child learns the use of the senses, the sensory knowledge, the perception of things which surround him, as later he acquires the analogous mechanism of transference which is linked with reading, or the new sensibility which accompanies the handling of tools, so the love of God involves an apprenticeship. A child knows at first that each letter corresponds to a sound. Later, by glancing at a page, the sound of a word comes directly to his mind through the eyes. Just so we begin at first abstractly to know that we must love God in all things. Only later the beloved presence of God, through all the incidents great or small which make up the stuff of each day, enters at each second into the centre of our soul. The passage to this state is an operation analogous to that by which a child learns to read, by which an apprentice learns his trade, but analogous above all to that by which a very young child learns the perception of sensible things.

We give to very young children, to help them, objects of a regular form and easy to handle, to explore, to recognize, such as balls and cubes. So, too, God facilitates men's apprenticeship by giving them, in social life, religious practices and the sacraments, and in the inanimate universe, beauty.

All human life, the most common life, the most natural, is made thus. As soon as we analyse it, we find a tissue of mysteries completely impenetrable to the intelligence. These are images of supernatural mysteries of which we can have an idea only by means of this resemblance.

Human thought and the universe constitute the books of revelation *par excellence*, if the attention, lighted by love and faith, knows how to decipher them. The reading of them is a proof, and indeed the only certain proof. After having read the *Iliad* in Greek, no one would dream of wondering whether the professor who taught him the Greek alphabet had deceived him.

XII

A SKETCH OF A HISTORY OF GREEK SCIENCE[1]

GREEK SCIENCE had its beginning in the idea of similar triangles attributed to Thales. Thales, who came of a half Phoenician family, was the master of Anaximander, a fragment of whose work cited earlier shows its inspiration to be the same as that which inspired the Pythagoreans. According to an ancient text, Thales and Pherecydes (the Syrian philosopher, perhaps Pythagoras' teacher, who said: 'Zeus, when he was on the point of creating, transformed himself into Love') established water as the principle of all things. But the ancient text adds that Pherecydes called that principle Chaos. If the primal water of Thales is identical with Chaos, then this is exactly the conception of the first lines of Genesis.

Similar triangles are triangles with proportional sides $\frac{a}{b}=\frac{c}{d}=\frac{e}{f}$. If two similar triangles have two equal sides, without however being congruent, one has a proportion in three terms, two extreme terms, and one mediator term: $\frac{a}{b}=\frac{b}{c}$.

If the problem is set: to construct a triangle which may be divided into two similar triangles having one common side, one

[1] From *Les Intuitions Préchrétiennes*, pages 173-180.

arrives at a construction of the right-angled triangle, which immediately gives the so-called theorem of Pythagoras (the sum of the squares of the other two sides is equal to the square of the hypotenuse), and the theorem posits the height of the right-angled triangle as the geometric mean between the segments determined on the hypotenuse. The theorem of the right-angled triangle inscribed in a circle is what makes the value of the circle for the construction of geometric means. In fact, these theorems have followed from those which concern similar triangles.

It is said that the notion of similar triangles permitted Thales to measure the height of the Egyptian pyramids by their shadows and the relationship or ratio between the height and the shadow of a man at the same hour. Thus proportion makes things measurable, and there follows, in a sense comprehensible for man, the forbidden dimension, that would lead to heaven: height. It is also similar triangles which made possible the measurement of the distances of the stars.

Furthermore, these theorems gave rise to the finding of a mean proportional between any two whole numbers.

The question arose whether this search for a geometric mean could be made either by arithmetic, or by a geometrical construction, or indeed by geometry alone? It is easy to show that the mean between one and two has a ratio or relationship with unity such that one cannot find any two whole numbers whatever united by this relationship or ratio. For the whole number which is twice a square of the form $2n^2$, can never be a square. The duplication of the square can only be accomplished by the geometrical construction of a geometric mean. One can also easily demonstrate that this holds for the mean between one and any non-squared number, as for the mean between one and two.

Thus these means, whatever they may count for among numbers, have no other than a geometrical support. After that was determined, it was necessary to establish that one can rigorously define the arithmetical operations and proportions of these quantities.

It is exactly this which is perfectly demonstrated by Euclid's Book V, whose material is attributed to Eudoxus, Plato's friend and the pupil of the Pythagorean geometrician Archytas. This book contains, in its perfected state, the theory which we today call the theory of real numbers. After the destruction of Greek civilization this theory was lost, even though we always possessed Euclid, simply because no one could understand the state of mind to which it corresponded. During the course of the last half century, mathematicians, having rediscovered the need for rigour, re-invented this theory, for none knew that it was to be had in Euclid; that was realized afterwards.

The essential point of this theory is a simple definition of proportion by means of ideas of the greater and smaller. It is said that a is to b as c is to d if $ma > {}^1nb$ always implies $mc > nd$, and if $ma < nd$ always implies $mc < nd$, whatever the whole m and n may be. It is easy to demonstrate that this condition is realized for similar triangles. Henceforth it is permissible to affirm in all rigour that the altitude of a right-angled triangle is the mean proportional between the segments of the hypotenuse.

Thus the relation (or ratio), which one may also name number, provided a real number is thereby understood, is defined only by an order of correspondence which mutually links four sets of an infinity of terms. The number or relation (ἀριθμός or λόγος) appears indeed as a mediation between unity and that which is unlimited.

In Plato's time also, the Oracle of Apollo, by giving the command to double the cubic temple of Delos, set before the Greek geometricians the problem of the duplication of the cube. This leads back to the search for two geometric mean proportionals between 2 and 1 $\left(\dfrac{2}{a} = \dfrac{a}{b} = \dfrac{b}{1}\right)$. Menaechmus, Plato's pupil, brought this search to its conclusion. Further, he is the inventor of the parabola and of the equilateral hyperbola. It is by the

---

[1] $a > 6 = a$ greater than 6
$a < 6 = a$ less than 6

intersection of these curves that he worked out the doubling of the cube. Now, if one takes the problem of finding two mean proportionals by focusing the attention upon the construction suitable for finding such a mean, by the use of the circle, one reaches a construction of the parabola as a conic section which includes its algebraic formula or equation. It is not at all improbable that Menaechmus should have found the conic sections with their formulas in seeking two mean proportionals between 1 and 2. He would in this way have invented the idea of function. In speaking here of formulas, I do not intend to speak of the combinations of letters which exist in our algebra, but of the knowledge of the variable relations of quantities which we express by these combinations, and which the Greeks did not express as we do, but did nevertheless clearly conceive. They possessed the idea of function. It appears in the history of their sciences linked with the search for the mean proportional. The first function found, which is the equation of the parabola, is the function which is the proportional mean between a variable and a constant.

The invention of integral calculus is attributed to the same Eudoxus who formulated the theory of real number. He also formulated the postulate wrongly known as the axiom of Archimedes. Here it is: 'Two quantities are said to be unequal when their difference added to itself can surpass all finite quantity.' This is the idea of the summing up of an unlimited series. By the use of this notion, Eudoxus found the volume of the pyramid and of the cone, and later Archimedes found the square of the parabola. It is therefore indeed a question of integration. A parabolic area is measured by the sum $1 + \frac{1}{4} + \frac{1}{4^2} + \frac{1}{4^3} + \ldots + \frac{1}{4^n} + \ldots$ The question thus concerns the sum of the terms of an infinite geometric progression. By the postulate called the axiom of Archimedes, one demonstrates that this sum is rigorously equal to $1 + \frac{1}{3}$. Apparent here is the mixture of limit and of that which is limitless. The same thing appears as unlimited and as finite. This was already the case in what is mistakenly named the paradoxes of Zeno.

Again it was Eudoxus who elaborated a system of astronomy in reply to Plato, who asked: 'Find the set of uniform circular motions which permit us to account for the movements of the planets. This is based on the ingenious idea of composite movements which is the basis of our mechanics. As we construct the parabolic movement of projectiles with two movements at right angles, one uniform the other accelerated, so Eudoxus gave account of all the positions of the stars known in his time by postulating several uniform circular motions simultaneously accomplished around different axes by each individual star. This conception is as bold and as pure as that which defines real number, or as that of the summing up of an unlimited series. If Plato wanted only uniform circular movements, that is because only such are divine, and because the stars, he said, are images of the divinity sculptured by divinity itself. Plato almost certainly had in mind this composite of movement when he spoke of the Other, rebellious to unity, harmonized by constraint with the Same. The sun, in its unique movement, is drawn at once by the circle of the equator and by that of the ecliptic, which corresponds to the Same and to the Other, it has but a single motion.

In the following period of Greek Science, Ptolemy reproduced Eudoxus' system in a much cruder form, Apollonius continued Menaechmus' discoveries concerning conics and Archimedes continued those of Eudoxus on the subject of integration.

Further, Archimedes founded mechanics and physics, that branch of mechanics which is called statics and is found nearly complete in his work, the theory of balance or leverage—it amounts to the same thing—and the theory of the centre of gravity, which springs from the first. The theory of balance, which with him is rigorously geometric, rests entirely upon proportion. There is equilibrium when the relation or ratio between the weights is the inverse of the relation or ratio between the distances from those weights to the point of support. This is why the liturgy can, in all strictness, say that the Cross was a scale whereon the body of Christ acted as counterpoise to the weight of the world. For Christ belonged to heaven, and the distance of heaven to the point of intersection of the branches of the Cross is the distance from this point to the earth, as the weight of the world to that of the body of Christ. Archimedes said: 'Give me a fulcrum and I will lift up the world.'

To carry out this boast two conditions were needed. First, that fulcrum itself should not belong to this world. Then, that this fulcrum should be at a finite distance from the centre of the world and at an infinite distance from the hand which acts. The operation of lifting the world by means of a lever is impossible except to God. The Incarnation supplies the fulcrum. Every sacrament is such a fulcrum. And that every human being who perfectly obeys God is such a fulcrum. For he is in the world but not of the world. He disposes of an infinitely small amount of power by comparison with the universe, but by obedience, the point of application of this force is carried through heaven. One may say that God acts here below in this manner only, that is, only by means of the infinitely small who, although being opposed to the infinitely great, are effective by means of the law of leverage.

Archimedes founded the science of physics by elaborating one of its branches, that is, hydrostatics. He constructed it in a purely geometric manner and without the least mixture of empiricism. This is a marvel which rests entirely upon proportion. When a body floats, the load-water line is such that the relation or ratio of the immersed volume to the total volume is identical to the relation between the density of the body and that of the water. This demonstrates itself as a theorem of geometry, by symmetry, after one has postulated that there is symmetry wherever there is equilibrium. Water thus appears as the perfect scale. This property which relates water to justice is perhaps not unconnected with the symbolism of baptism in its primary form. A man immersed submits to two attractions, one toward the depth, the other toward the height, and the latter carries him away.

Almost nothing is known about the fundamentals of chemistry as understood in ancient times, except that in Plato there is a theory of the four elements founded upon proportion. Air and water are two mean proportionals between fire—which is also light and energy—and the earth. To sum up, there is energy, matter and two mean proportionals which relate them. Two because space is three-dimensional.

Biology was already far advanced in Plato's time, since Hippocrates is earlier than Plato. Biology was principally founded upon the ideas of proportion and of harmony as the unity of contraries. Hippocrates defined health as a certain proportion in the pairs of contraries which concern the living body, such as cold and warmth, dryness and humidity, a proportion which should respond to the physical environment: and so, by the process of elimination, the living being is the image of the environment.

CPSIA information can be obtained
at www.ICGtesting.com
Printed in the USA
BVHW030013211219
567397BV00001B/3/P

9 780415 186629